Mastering Data Structures and Algorithms with C++

A Step-by-Step Guide to Advanced Programming Concepts and Techniques

MIGUEL FARMER

RAFAEL SANDERS

Table of Content

TABLE OF CONTENTS

INTRODUCTION

Welcome to **Mastering Data Structures and Algorithms with C++: A Step-by-Step Guide to Advanced Programming Concepts and Techniques**. This book is designed to provide a comprehensive understanding of data structures and algorithms, with a focus on their implementation and optimization in C++. Whether you're a beginner eager to dive into the world of programming or an experienced developer looking to sharpen your skills, this guide will equip you with the knowledge to tackle a wide range of complex programming challenges.

In today's fast-paced technological landscape, the ability to design efficient algorithms and choose the appropriate data structures is crucial. The performance and scalability of software systems often depend on how well these foundational concepts are applied. This book aims to not only teach you the theoretical aspects of algorithms and data structures but also show you how to apply them practically using C++, one of the most powerful and widely used programming languages in both industry and academia.

Why C++?

C++ remains a go-to language for systems programming, game development, and performance-critical applications due to its ability to provide a balance between low-level memory control and high-level abstractions. The language's rich set of features, such as object-oriented programming (OOP), templates, and the Standard Template Library (STL), makes it an ideal choice for implementing complex algorithms and data structures. Throughout this book, we'll leverage C++ to demonstrate efficient implementations, focusing on practical, real-world applications.

A Journey Through Data Structures and Algorithms

This book is organized into multiple sections, each focusing on a different aspect of data structures and algorithms. We begin with foundational concepts, gradually advancing to more complex techniques and real-world applications. You'll gain a deep understanding of the following key areas:

Part 1: Foundations of Programming and Algorithms

- We start by introducing the basics of **C++ programming**, including variables, data types, and control structures. You'll get a solid foundation in C++ syntax, enabling you to move on to more advanced topics with ease.
- The core of this section lays the groundwork for data structures and algorithms, covering fundamental topics such as **pointers, memory management**, and **object-oriented programming (OOP)**. Understanding these topics will help you make the most of C++'s powerful

features when building efficient data structures and algorithms.

Part 2: Essential Data Structures

- This part explores key data structures such as **arrays, linked lists, stacks, queues, hash tables**, and **trees**. You'll learn not only how to implement these structures but also how to choose the right one based on specific problem requirements.
- We will also discuss the **Standard Template Library (STL)**, a powerful collection of classes and functions in C++ that provides built-in support for many of these data structures.

Part 3: Advanced Algorithms and Problem Solving

- Building on the data structures from Part 2, this section covers advanced algorithmic techniques. You'll learn about **sorting** and **searching algorithms**, including classic algorithms like **quick sort, merge sort**, and **binary search**, as well as more advanced techniques like **dynamic programming** and **greedy algorithms**.
- Key to this section is the understanding of algorithm optimization and its real-world applications. The focus is not just on solving problems but solving them efficiently,

ensuring that your solutions are scalable and suitable for large data sets.

Part 4: Advanced Topics and Optimization Techniques

- As you gain confidence in basic algorithms and data structures, this section introduces more advanced topics such as **suffix arrays**, **segment trees**, and **Fenwick trees**. These structures provide solutions to complex problems and are often used in applications involving text processing, range queries, and real-time updates.

- Optimization techniques, including **amortized analysis**, **parallelism**, and **concurrency**, will show you how to take full advantage of modern processors and multi-threaded environments, making your code faster and more scalable.

Part 5: Real-World Applications

- Finally, this book delves into **real-world applications** of the algorithms and data structures you've learned. From **machine learning** and **game development** to **networking** and **system design**, you'll see how to apply these concepts to solve practical problems in a variety of fields.

- We'll walk through several project-based examples, illustrating how to build and implement complex systems and optimize them for real-world performance.

Learning Through Practice

This book takes a **hands-on approach** to learning. Each concept is followed by **practical examples** and **exercises** to reinforce your understanding. You will be encouraged to implement algorithms from scratch, experiment with different data structures, and solve real-world problems using C++. By the end of this book, you will not only have learned the theoretical aspects of computer science but will also be comfortable implementing them in C++ and optimizing your solutions for real-world applications.

Debugging and Troubleshooting

An integral part of programming is **debugging** and **troubleshooting**. As you work through the exercises and projects in this book, you'll encounter errors and challenges. Learning how to troubleshoot and debug is an essential skill, and we will provide you with strategies to help you identify and fix issues efficiently. C++ debugging tools, best practices for error handling, and methods for testing and profiling your code will be discussed throughout the book.

Why This Book?

The purpose of **Mastering Data Structures and Algorithms with C++** is to provide a complete, in-depth resource for anyone interested in mastering algorithms and data structures. Unlike other books that may skim over advanced topics or focus only on theoretical aspects, this book ensures that you understand the practical application of each algorithm. You'll see how to implement these algorithms in C++ step-by-step, understand the trade-offs between different approaches, and apply them in real-world scenarios.

Whether you're preparing for technical interviews, working on academic projects, or simply enhancing your programming skills, this book will serve as a comprehensive reference guide to help you succeed. We've designed it to be suitable for readers of all skill levels, providing foundational knowledge while also challenging more advanced programmers with complex problems and optimizations.

Conclusion

By the end of this book, you will have gained a thorough understanding of algorithms and data structures and how to implement and optimize them using C++. You'll be able to apply this knowledge to real-world challenges in fields ranging from software engineering and machine learning to game development and networking.

The ability to choose the right algorithm and data structure for a given problem is a fundamental skill for any programmer. Armed with the insights and practical skills you'll gain from this book, you'll be ready to take on complex programming challenges with confidence and efficiency.

Let's get started on this journey of mastering data structures, algorithms, and C++!

CHAPTER 1

INTRODUCTION TO C++ PROGRAMMING

This chapter will introduce C++ programming and provide the foundational knowledge needed to start working with data structures and algorithms. It is aimed at beginners but will include enough depth for more experienced developers to benefit as well.

Overview of C++

C++ is a powerful, high-performance programming language used in a variety of applications, from system software to games and high-performance applications. It was developed by Bjarne Stroustrup in 1979 and is an extension of the C language, adding object-oriented programming (OOP) features.

Key features of C++ include:

- **Object-Oriented Programming (OOP)**: C++ supports classes, inheritance, polymorphism, and encapsulation.
- **Efficiency**: C++ allows fine-grained control over system resources, making it ideal for performance-critical applications.

- **Rich Standard Library**: The C++ Standard Library includes collections of pre-built classes and functions, making development faster and easier.

C++ is one of the most widely used programming languages today, especially in systems programming, game development, embedded systems, and performance-critical software.

Setting Up a Development Environment

Before you start coding in C++, you'll need to set up a development environment. Here's a step-by-step guide for setting up your environment on different platforms:

- **Windows**:
    - o Install an Integrated Development Environment (IDE) such as **Code::Blocks** or **Microsoft Visual Studio**.
    - o Alternatively, you can install **MinGW** (Minimalist GNU for Windows) and use **GCC (GNU Compiler Collection)** for compiling C++ code from the command line.
- **MacOS**:
    - o Install **Xcode** from the Mac App Store, which includes all the necessary tools and compilers.
    - o You can also use a lightweight IDE like **CLion** or **Visual Studio Code** for C++ development.

- **Linux**:
  - o Most Linux distributions come with **GCC** pre-installed. You can install it if it's not already installed via the package manager (e.g., `sudo apt-get install build-essential`).
  - o IDEs such as **Eclipse**, **CLion**, or **Visual Studio Code** are also popular choices for C++ development.

Once the environment is set up, you should be able to create and run C++ programs from the terminal or IDE.

Basic Syntax and First Program

To write a basic C++ program, you need to understand the syntax. Here's a simple example of a "Hello, World!" program, which is often the first program written by beginners in any language:

```cpp
cpp

#include <iostream> // This line includes the input/output stream

int main() {
    std::cout << "Hello, World!"; // Prints "Hello, World!" to the console
    return 0; // Exits the program with a success status
```

15

```
}
```

Key parts of the program:

- `#include <iostream>`: This tells the compiler to include the input-output stream library, which contains functions for output like `std::cout`.
- `int main()`: The `main` function is where execution starts. In C++, the program always starts running from the `main` function.
- `std::cout << "Hello, World!";`: This line prints the message to the console.
- `return 0;`: The `main` function ends by returning an integer. `0` indicates that the program has run successfully.

C++ Essentials for Data Structures and Algorithms

Before diving into data structures and algorithms, it's important to understand some essential C++ features that are fundamental to efficient coding. These will serve as building blocks when implementing algorithms and working with data structures:

1. **Variables and Data Types**: Understanding how to declare variables and choose the appropriate data type (e.g., `int`, `double`, `char`, `bool`, `string`) is crucial. Data structures will depend heavily on these types.

2. **Control Structures**: Conditional statements (`if`, `else`, `switch`) and looping mechanisms (`for`, `while`, `do-while`) allow you to control the flow of your program. You'll use these to navigate through elements in data structures.

3. **Functions**: Functions are used to break a program into smaller, reusable pieces of code. You will use functions to implement algorithms for manipulating data structures. For example, sorting, searching, and traversing will be organized into functions.

4. **Pointers and References**: Understanding how C++ handles memory through pointers and references is crucial for efficient algorithm design. For example, pointers will be used to dynamically allocate memory for data structures such as arrays and linked lists.

5. **Object-Oriented Programming (OOP)**: As C++ is an object-oriented language, understanding classes and objects, along with concepts like inheritance and polymorphism, is essential when implementing more complex data structures (e.g., trees, graphs) and algorithms (e.g., graph traversal, sorting).

By the end of this chapter, you'll be familiar with the basic building blocks of C++ and how they apply to data structures and algorithms. This understanding will make it easier to grasp more advanced topics in later chapters.

CHAPTER 2

UNDERSTANDING VARIABLES, DATA TYPES, AND CONTROL STRUCTURES

This chapter will cover the essential components of C++ programming, such as variables, data types, conditionals, loops, and functions. These foundational concepts will help you write efficient and organized code, which is crucial when working with data structures and algorithms.

Variables and Data Types in C++

In C++, a variable is a storage location associated with a data type that holds a value. Understanding how to declare and use variables is fundamental to writing effective programs. Variables must be declared before use, specifying their type, which determines the kind of data they can hold.

Basic Data Types

- **int**: Used for storing integers (whole numbers), e.g., `int age = 25;`

- **float**: Used for storing single-precision floating-point numbers (decimals), e.g., `float height = 5.9f;`
- **double**: Used for storing double-precision floating-point numbers, e.g., `double pi = 3.14159;`
- **char**: Used for storing a single character, e.g., `char grade = 'A';`
- **bool**: Used for storing boolean values, `true` or `false`, e.g., `bool isOpen = true;`
- **string**: A sequence of characters, e.g., `string name = "John Doe";` (Note: `string` requires the `#include <string>` header).

Example: Declaring Variables

cpp

```cpp
#include <iostream>
using namespace std;

int main() {
    int age = 30;  // integer variable
    float weight = 72.5f;   // floating point
number
    char grade = 'A';  // single character
    bool isStudent = true;  // boolean value
    string name = "John";   // string of
characters

    cout << "Name: " << name << "\n";
```

19

```
cout << "Age: " << age << "\n";
cout << "Weight: " << weight << "\n";
cout << "Grade: " << grade << "\n";
cout << "Is Student: " << isStudent << "\n";

return 0;
}
```

In this example, we declare several variables of different types and display their values.

Type Conversion (Casting)

C++ supports both **implicit** and **explicit** type conversion (casting). Implicit casting is done automatically by the compiler when converting from a smaller to a larger data type (e.g., int to float). Explicit casting is done manually when you need to convert from one type to another.

Example of explicit casting:

cpp

```
int x = 5;
float y = static_cast<float>(x);    // Explicit
cast from int to float
```

Conditionals and Loops

Conditionals and loops are fundamental control structures that allow you to make decisions and repeat tasks.

Conditionals

Conditionals allow you to execute a block of code only if a certain condition is true. The main conditional structures are `if`, `else if`, and `else`.

- **if**: Executes a block of code if a specified condition is true.
- **else if**: Used if the previous `if` condition is false but another condition needs to be checked.
- **else**: Executes a block of code if no previous condition is true.

Example:

cpp

```cpp
int age = 18;
if (age >= 18) {
    cout << "You are an adult.\n";
} else {
    cout << "You are a minor.\n";
}
```

21

Switch-Case

If you have multiple possible conditions, the `switch` statement is more efficient than using multiple `if-else` blocks.

Example:

cpp

```cpp
int day = 2;
switch(day) {
    case 1: cout << "Monday"; break;
    case 2: cout << "Tuesday"; break;
    case 3: cout << "Wednesday"; break;
    default: cout << "Invalid day"; break;
}
```

Loops

Loops allow you to execute a block of code repeatedly based on a condition. The main types of loops are `for`, `while`, and `do-while`.

- **for**: Useful when you know how many times you want to repeat the code.
- **while**: Repeats the code as long as a condition is true.
- **do-while**: Executes the code at least once, then checks the condition.

Example:

cpp

```cpp
// for loop example
for (int i = 0; i < 5; i++) {
    cout << "i = " << i << "\n";
}


// while loop example
int j = 0;
while (j < 5) {
    cout << "j = " << j << "\n";
    j++;
}


// do-while loop example
int k = 0;
do {
    cout << "k = " << k << "\n";
    k++;
} while (k < 5);
```

Functions and Modular Programming

In C++, functions allow you to organize your code into smaller, reusable blocks. Functions can be used to implement algorithms and perform specific tasks, making your code more modular and easier to understand and maintain.

Defining Functions

A function in C++ is defined with a return type, name, and parameters (if any). The function body contains the statements to be executed.

Example:

cpp

```cpp
#include <iostream>
using namespace std;

// Function declaration
int add(int a, int b);

int main() {
    int result = add(5, 3);   // Calling the add function
    cout << "The sum is: " << result << "\n";
    return 0;
}

// Function definition
int add(int a, int b) {
    return a + b;
}
```

In this example, we define a function called `add` that takes two integers, adds them, and returns the result. This function is called inside the `main` function, and the result is displayed.

Function Overloading

C++ supports **function overloading**, where you can define multiple functions with the same name but different parameter types or numbers.

Example:

cpp

```cpp
#include <iostream>
using namespace std;

int add(int a, int b) {
    return a + b;
}

double add(double a, double b) {
    return a + b;
}

int main() {
    cout << add(2, 3) << "\n"; // Calls the
integer version
```

```cpp
    cout << add(2.5, 3.5) << "\n"; // Calls the
double version
    return 0;
}
```

Return Types and Parameters

- Functions can return values (e.g., int, float, void for no return).
- Functions can take parameters to perform operations based on input values.

Example with multiple parameters:

cpp

```cpp
int multiply(int x, int y) {
    return x * y;
}

int main() {
    int result = multiply(4, 5);
    cout << "Product: " << result << "\n";
    return 0;
}
```

In this example, the function multiply takes two integer parameters and returns their product.

Recursive Functions

Recursion is a technique where a function calls itself. It's often used in algorithms that involve breaking a problem into smaller subproblems (e.g., in tree traversal or solving problems like factorials).

Example:

cpp

```cpp
int factorial(int n) {
    if (n <= 1) return 1;
    return n * factorial(n - 1);
}

int main() {
    cout << factorial(5); // Outputs 120
    return 0;
}
```

This function calculates the factorial of a number using recursion.

Summary of Key Concepts:

- **Variables and Data Types**: Learn how to declare and use different data types (int, float, char, bool, string).

- **Conditionals and Loops**: Use `if`, `else if`, `else`, `switch`, and looping constructs like `for`, `while`, and `do-while` to control the flow of your program.

- **Functions**: Break your program into reusable functions to simplify your code and improve maintainability. Learn how to define, call, and use functions, including function overloading and recursion.

These basic concepts are foundational for writing effective programs in C++ and will play a crucial role in understanding more complex data structures and algorithms. Let me know if you'd like further details or code examples on any of these topics!

CHAPTER 3

POINTERS, REFERENCES, AND MEMORY MANAGEMENT

This chapter covers the concept of pointers, references, and memory management in C++, which are fundamental to writing efficient, high-performance code. Understanding these concepts is especially crucial when working with dynamic data structures such as linked lists, trees, and graphs, which require dynamic memory allocation.

Introduction to Pointers and Memory Addresses

A **pointer** in C++ is a variable that holds the **memory address** of another variable. Unlike regular variables, which store values, pointers store the locations in memory where data is located.

Basic Pointer Concept

In C++, a pointer is declared using an asterisk (*) before the pointer's name. The pointer will hold the address of the variable to which it points.

Syntax:

cpp

```
type* pointerName;
```

- **type**: Specifies the data type the pointer will point to (e.g., int, char, etc.)
- *****: Indicates that this variable is a pointer.

Example:

cpp

```cpp
int num = 10;    // Declare an integer variable
int* ptr = &num; // Declare a pointer to int and
store the address of num

cout << "Value of num: " << num << "\n";          //
Output: 10
cout << "Address of num: " << &num << "\n";       //
Output: memory address
cout << "Value stored in ptr: " << ptr << "\n";
// Output: same as address of num
cout << "Dereferencing ptr: " << *ptr << "\n";
// Output: 10 (value at the address)
```

Key Concepts:

- **Dereferencing (*ptr)**: This operator accesses the value stored at the memory address pointed to by the pointer. In the above example, *ptr returns the value of num, which is 10.

- **Address-of Operator (&)**: This operator is used to get the memory address of a variable. In the example above, &num gives the memory address where num is stored.

Pointer Arithmetic

C++ allows you to perform arithmetic on pointers. When you increment a pointer, it moves to the next memory location of the type it points to.

Example:

cpp

```
int arr[] = {10, 20, 30};
int* ptr = arr;

cout << *ptr << "\n";    // Output: 10
ptr++;                   // Increment the pointer
cout << *ptr << "\n";    // Output: 20
```

Dynamic Memory Allocation

Dynamic memory allocation allows the program to allocate memory at runtime, which is particularly useful when dealing with dynamic data structures (e.g., linked lists, dynamic arrays). In C++, the new keyword is used to allocate memory, and the delete keyword is used to deallocate memory when it is no longer needed.

Using new for Memory Allocation

The new operator allocates memory on the heap and returns a pointer to that memory.

Example:

cpp

```cpp
int* ptr = new int;    // Allocate memory for one integer
*ptr = 5;              // Assign value to allocated memory

cout << "Value: " << *ptr << "\n";   // Output: 5

delete ptr;            // Free the allocated memory
```

Allocating Arrays Dynamically

You can also use new to allocate memory for an array of elements.

Example:

cpp

```cpp
int* arr = new int[5]; // Allocate memory for an array of 5 integers

// Assigning values to array elements
```

```
for (int i = 0; i < 5; i++) {
    arr[i] = i * 2;
    cout << arr[i] << " ";   // Output: 0 2 4 6 8
}


delete[] arr;   // Free the memory allocated for
the array
```

- **delete[]**: Used to deallocate memory allocated for arrays.
- **delete**: Used to deallocate memory allocated for a single variable.

Common Pitfalls in Memory Management

- **Memory Leaks**: Occurs when memory is allocated but never deallocated.
- **Dangling Pointers**: A pointer that continues to reference a memory location after it has been deallocated.
- **Double Deletion**: Deleting the same memory location more than once.

To avoid these issues, always ensure that every call to `new` is matched with a call to `delete`.

Smart Pointers and Memory Management in C++

C++ provides **smart pointers** as part of the Standard Library to help manage memory automatically and prevent common issues like memory leaks and dangling pointers. Smart pointers use **RAII (Resource Acquisition Is Initialization)**, which ensures that resources (like memory) are automatically released when they are no longer needed.

Types of Smart Pointers in C++

1. **std::unique_ptr**: Represents ownership of a resource. Only one `unique_ptr` can own the resource at a time. When the `unique_ptr` goes out of scope, it automatically deletes the resource.

   Example:

   cpp

   ```cpp
   #include <memory>
   using namespace std;

   int main() {
       unique_ptr<int>         ptr         =
   make_unique<int>(10);
       cout << *ptr << "\n"; // Output: 10
   ```

```
// No need to call delete; the memory
is freed automatically when ptr goes out of
scope
}
```

2. **std::shared_ptr**: Allows multiple shared_ptr objects to share ownership of the same resource. The resource is only deleted when the last shared_ptr that owns it is destroyed.

Example:

cpp

```
#include <memory>
using namespace std;

int main() {
    shared_ptr<int>           ptr1          =
make_shared<int>(20);
    shared_ptr<int> ptr2 = ptr1; // ptr2
shares ownership with ptr1
    cout << *ptr1 << "\n"; // Output: 20
    cout << *ptr2 << "\n"; // Output: 20
    // Memory is freed automatically when
both ptr1 and ptr2 go out of scope
}
```

3. **std::weak_ptr**: Used to break circular references between shared_ptr objects. It does not affect the reference count, meaning it can be used to observe an object managed by shared_ptr without owning it.

Example:

cpp

```cpp
#include <memory>
using namespace std;

int main() {
    shared_ptr<int>          sp          =
make_shared<int>(30);
    weak_ptr<int> wp = sp;  // wp is a weak
reference to sp
    if (auto locked = wp.lock()) {    //
Check if the shared pointer still exists
        cout  <<  *locked  <<  "\n";    //
Output: 30
    }
}
```

When to Use Smart Pointers

- Use **unique_ptr** when a resource should have only one owner.
- Use **shared_ptr** when multiple parts of your program need to share ownership of a resource.

- Use **weak_ptr** to observe a resource without preventing its deletion.

Advantages of Smart Pointers

- Automatic memory management prevents memory leaks and dangling pointers.
- Helps prevent complex bugs related to manual memory management.
- Simplifies resource management in larger, more complex applications.

Summary of Key Concepts:

- **Pointers**: Variables that store memory addresses. They are essential for dynamic memory management and working with data structures like linked lists.
- **Memory Addresses**: The actual location in memory where data is stored. You can access and manipulate memory directly using pointers.
- **Dynamic Memory Allocation**: Allows for memory allocation at runtime using the `new` keyword, and deallocation using `delete`.
- **Smart Pointers**: Use `std::unique_ptr`, `std::shared_ptr`, and `std::weak_ptr` for automatic and safer memory management, avoiding common pitfalls like memory leaks and dangling pointers.

Mastering pointers and memory management is essential for writing efficient C++ code, especially when dealing with large datasets or complex data structures. Let me know if you need further clarification or additional examples!

CHAPTER 4

OBJECT-ORIENTED PROGRAMMING IN C++

In this chapter, we'll dive into **Object-Oriented Programming (OOP)** concepts in C++, which are essential for building maintainable, scalable, and reusable code. C++ supports OOP principles like **encapsulation**, **inheritance**, **polymorphism**, and **abstraction**, which are vital when implementing complex data structures and algorithms.

Classes and Objects

In C++, a **class** is a blueprint or template for creating objects. It defines the properties (data) and behaviors (functions) that the objects of that class will have. An **object** is an instance of a class.

Defining a Class

A class is defined using the `class` keyword, followed by its name and a block of code that defines its attributes (variables) and methods (functions).

Example:

cpp

```cpp
#include <iostream>
using namespace std;

class Car {
public:
    // Attributes
    string make;
    string model;
    int year;

    // Method (function)
    void start() {
        cout << "The " << make << " " << model <<
" is starting." << endl;
    }

    void stop() {
        cout << "The " << make << " " << model <<
" has stopped." << endl;
    }
};

int main() {
    Car myCar;   // Creating an object of the Car
class
    myCar.make   =   "Toyota";     //   Accessing
attributes
    myCar.model = "Corolla";
```

```
    myCar.year = 2020;

    myCar.start();   // Calling a method
    myCar.stop();

    return 0;
}
```

In this example:

- `Car` is a class.
- `myCar` is an object of the `Car` class.
- We use the . (dot) operator to access the attributes and methods of an object.

Constructors and Destructors

A **constructor** is a special function that is called automatically when an object of a class is created. It is used to initialize the object's attributes. A **destructor** is used to clean up resources when an object is destroyed.

Example:

cpp

```
class Car {
public:
    string make;
```

41

```cpp
    string model;
    int year;

    // Constructor
    Car(string m, string mo, int y) {
        make = m;
        model = mo;
        year = y;
    }

    // Destructor
    ~Car() {
        cout << "The " << make << " " << model <<
" is being destroyed." << endl;
    }

    void start() {
        cout << "The " << make << " " << model <<
" is starting." << endl;
    }
};

int main() {
    Car myCar("Toyota", "Corolla", 2020);    //
Constructor initializes attributes
    myCar.start();

    // Destructor is automatically called when
myCar goes out of scope
```

```
    return 0;
}
```

In this example, the constructor initializes the attributes `make`, `model`, and `year` when the object is created. The destructor is automatically called when the object goes out of scope, which is useful for resource management.

Encapsulation, Inheritance, and Polymorphism

These three concepts form the core of object-oriented design in C++.

Encapsulation

Encapsulation is the practice of keeping fields (data) private and providing access to them through public methods (getters and setters). This helps ensure that the internal representation of the object is hidden from outside interference and misuse.

Example:

cpp

```cpp
class Car {
private:
    string make;
    string model;
    int year;
```

```cpp
public:
    // Setter function for make
    void setMake(string m) {
        make = m;
    }

    // Getter function for make
    string getMake() {
        return make;
    }

    // Method to display car info
    void displayInfo() {
        cout << "Car: " << make << " " << model
<< " (" << year << ")" << endl;
    }
};

int main() {
    Car myCar;
    myCar.setMake("Toyota");  // Using setter
    myCar.displayInfo();       // Using getter to
access make
    return 0;
}
```

In this example, the data members `make`, `model`, and `year` are **private** to the class, and can only be accessed through public setter and getter functions. This protects the integrity of the data.

Inheritance

Inheritance allows one class to derive the properties and behaviors (methods) of another class. It promotes code reuse and hierarchical classification.

Example:

cpp

```cpp
class Vehicle {
public:
    void start() {
        cout << "Vehicle is starting." << endl;
    }
};

class Car : public Vehicle {   // Car inherits
from Vehicle
public:
    void honk() {
        cout << "Car is honking." << endl;
    }
};
```

```cpp
int main() {
    Car myCar;
    myCar.start();    // Inherited method from Vehicle
    myCar.honk();    // Method from Car
    return 0;
}
```

In this example, `Car` is a subclass that inherits from the `Vehicle` class. The `Car` class can use the `start()` method of the `Vehicle` class and also has its own `honk()` method.

Polymorphism

Polymorphism allows objects of different classes to be treated as objects of a common base class. The most common use of polymorphism is with **virtual functions**, which allow derived classes to override base class methods.

Example (Runtime Polymorphism using Virtual Functions):

cpp

```cpp
class Animal {
public:
    virtual void speak() {    // Virtual function
        cout << "Animal is making a sound." << endl;
    }
```

```
};


class Dog : public Animal {
public:
    void speak() override {   // Overriding the
base class function
        cout << "Dog is barking." << endl;
    }
};


int main() {
    Animal* animalPtr;
    Dog myDog;

    animalPtr = &myDog;
    animalPtr->speak();   // Calls Dog's speak()
function (runtime polymorphism)

    return 0;
}
```

In this example:

- The speak() function is declared as virtual in the base class Animal. This means that C++ will look at the type of the object at runtime and call the correct version of the function (Dog::speak() in this case), even if the pointer is of type Animal*.

- This is **runtime polymorphism**, where the method to be called is determined during the program's execution.

Abstraction and Interfaces

Abstraction involves hiding complex implementation details and exposing only the necessary parts of an object or function. In C++, abstraction is typically achieved through **abstract classes** and **interfaces**.

Abstract Classes

An **abstract class** is a class that cannot be instantiated and typically contains at least one pure virtual function. Pure virtual functions are defined in the base class but must be implemented in derived classes.

Example:

cpp

```
class Shape {
public:
    virtual void draw() = 0;  // Pure virtual
function, making Shape abstract
};

class Circle : public Shape {
public:
```

```cpp
    void draw() override {
        cout << "Drawing a circle." << endl;
    }
};

int main() {
    // Shape shape;  // Error: Cannot instantiate abstract class
    Circle c;
    c.draw();  // Calls Circle's draw method
    return 0;
}
```

Here, the Shape class is abstract because it contains a pure virtual function draw(). Any class derived from Shape must provide an implementation of the draw() function.

Interfaces in C++

In C++, interfaces are commonly created by using **abstract classes** with only pure virtual functions. There is no direct interface keyword like in other languages, but abstract classes with pure virtual functions achieve the same result.

Example:

cpp

```cpp
class Drawable {
```

```
public:
    virtual void draw() = 0;   // Interface method
};

class Rectangle : public Drawable {
public:
    void draw() override {
        cout << "Drawing a rectangle." << endl;
    }
};

int main() {
    Drawable* drawable = new Rectangle();
    drawable->draw();   // Calls Rectangle's draw
method
    delete drawable;
    return 0;
}
```

Here, `Drawable` acts as an interface that specifies the contract for any drawable object to implement the `draw()` method.

Summary of Key Concepts:

- **Classes and Objects**: Classes define the structure and behavior of objects. Objects are instances of classes.
- **Encapsulation**: The practice of bundling data and methods together and restricting direct access to some of an object's components.

- **Inheritance**: A mechanism for creating a new class from an existing class, enabling reuse of code and establishing a hierarchy.

- **Polymorphism**: The ability to treat objects of different types through a common interface, typically using virtual functions.

- **Abstraction and Interfaces**: Hiding the implementation details and exposing only the necessary parts of an object. Abstract classes and interfaces are used to define contracts for derived classes.

Understanding and applying these OOP principles will allow you to design more modular, maintainable, and reusable C++ code, especially when working with complex data structures and algorithms. Let me know if you need more examples or clarifications on any topic!

CHAPTER 5

THE STANDARD TEMPLATE LIBRARY (STL) BASICS

The **Standard Template Library (STL)** is one of the most powerful features of C++. It provides a set of commonly used classes and functions that can significantly simplify development. The STL includes several container types (like arrays, lists, maps), algorithms for working with them, and iterators to access elements in a uniform way.

In this chapter, we will cover:

1. **Introduction to STL**: What it is and why it's useful.
2. **Containers**: Different types of containers in the STL.
3. **Iterators and Algorithms**: How to work with containers and use STL algorithms effectively.

Introduction to STL

The **Standard Template Library (STL)** is a collection of template classes and functions that provide common data structures and algorithms. It was designed to simplify code writing, improve code quality, and offer efficient data structures for both simple and complex tasks.

STL is based on the **generic programming paradigm**, meaning it allows you to create functions and classes that can work with any data type. This is achieved using **templates**, a feature in C++ that enables type-safe operations on data.

STL provides the following key components:

- **Containers**: Store data, e.g., `vector`, `list`, `map`, `set`.
- **Iterators**: Provide a way to access data in containers.
- **Algorithms**: Predefined functions that operate on containers, such as sorting, searching, etc.

Containers: Vectors, Lists, Maps, and Sets

The STL provides a variety of containers for different needs. Containers are template classes that hold data and provide member functions to access and manipulate that data.

Vectors

A **vector** is a dynamic array that can grow or shrink in size as needed. Vectors provide fast access to elements, but inserting or deleting elements in the middle of the vector can be costly because it requires shifting elements.

- **Dynamic Size**: Vectors automatically resize themselves when elements are added or removed.

- **Efficient Random Access**: Vectors allow for efficient access to elements by index.

Example:

cpp

```cpp
#include <iostream>
#include <vector>
using namespace std;

int main() {
    vector<int> numbers = {1, 2, 3, 4};    // Initialize a vector with values
    numbers.push_back(5);   // Add an element at the end

    for (int num : numbers) {  // Iterate using range-based for loop
        cout << num << " ";   // Output: 1 2 3 4 5
    }
    cout << endl;

    cout << "Size: " << numbers.size() << endl; // Output the size of the vector
    return 0;
}
```

Lists

A **list** is a doubly-linked list, which means each element contains pointers to the next and previous elements. It allows efficient insertion and deletion of elements at both ends, but accessing elements by index is slower compared to vectors because it requires traversal.

- **Efficient Insertions/Deletions**: Lists are better suited for frequent insertions and deletions.
- **No Random Access**: You can only traverse the list sequentially.

Example:

cpp

```cpp
#include <iostream>
#include <list>
using namespace std;

int main() {
    list<int> numbers = {10, 20, 30, 40};

    numbers.push_back(50);  // Add to the end of
the list
    numbers.push_front(5);  // Add to the front
of the list
```

```
    for (int num : numbers) {
        cout << num << " ";   // Output: 5 10 20
30 40 50
    }
    cout << endl;

    numbers.pop_front();    // Remove from the
front
    numbers.pop_back();   // Remove from the back

    for (int num : numbers) {
        cout << num << " ";   // Output: 10 20 30
40
    }
    cout << endl;

    return 0;
}
```

Maps

A **map** is an associative container that stores key-value pairs. Each element is a pair, where the key is unique. Maps provide fast lookups, insertions, and deletions based on the key.

- **Key-Value Pairs**: Each element is a pair consisting of a unique key and its associated value.
- **Ordered**: Maps store elements in sorted order based on the key.

Example:

cpp

```cpp
#include <iostream>
#include <map>
using namespace std;

int main() {
    map<string, int> age;
    age["Alice"] = 30;
    age["Bob"] = 25;
    age["Charlie"] = 35;

    // Iterate over the map
    for (const auto& pair : age) {
        cout << pair.first << " is " <<
pair.second << " years old." << endl;
    }
    return 0;
}
```

Sets

A **set** is a collection of unique elements stored in sorted order. Sets automatically discard duplicate values and allow for fast searching and insertion.

- **Unique Elements**: A set only stores unique elements.
- **Ordered**: Sets store elements in sorted order.

57

Example:

cpp

```cpp
#include <iostream>
#include <set>
using namespace std;

int main() {
    set<int> numbers = {1, 2, 3, 4, 5, 5, 4};  // Duplicates are removed

    numbers.insert(6);  // Add a new element to the set

    for (int num : numbers) {
        cout << num << " ";  // Output: 1 2 3 4 5 6
    }
    cout << endl;

    return 0;
}
```

Iterators and Algorithms

Iterators are used to traverse through containers and access their elements. STL provides different types of iterators, such as **forward iterators**, **bidirectional iterators**, and **random access iterators**, depending on the container type.

Iterators

An **iterator** is similar to a pointer in C++, providing access to elements in a container. You can use iterators to loop through elements in a container, which works for all types of containers in the STL.

Example (using iterators with a vector):

cpp

```cpp
#include <iostream>
#include <vector>
using namespace std;

int main() {
    vector<int> numbers = {1, 2, 3, 4, 5};
    vector<int>::iterator it = numbers.begin();
// Iterator to the first element

    // Using the iterator to traverse the vector
    while (it != numbers.end()) {
        cout << *it << " ";  // Dereferencing the
iterator to access the element
        ++it;  // Move to the next element
    }
    cout << endl;

    return 0;
```

```
}
```

Algorithms

STL algorithms provide commonly used functions to work with containers, such as sorting, searching, and manipulating elements. These algorithms are generic and can be used with any container that supports iterators.

Common STL algorithms:

- **sort()**: Sorts elements in ascending or descending order.
- **find()**: Searches for an element in a container.
- **reverse()**: Reverses the order of elements.
- **accumulate()**: Computes the sum of elements in a container.

Example (using algorithms):

cpp

```cpp
#include <iostream>
#include <vector>
#include <algorithm>  // For sort and find
using namespace std;

int main() {
    vector<int> numbers = {5, 3, 8, 1, 9};
```

```
    // Sort the vector
    sort(numbers.begin(), numbers.end());    //
Sort in ascending order

    for (int num : numbers) {
        cout << num << " ";   // Output: 1 3 5 8
9
    }
    cout << endl;

    // Search for an element
    auto    it    =    find(numbers.begin(),
numbers.end(), 5);
    if (it != numbers.end()) {
        cout << "Found 5!" << endl;
    }

    return 0;
}
```

In this example:

- **sort()** is used to sort the vector in ascending order.
- **find()** searches for the number 5 in the vector. If found, it returns an iterator to the element, otherwise it returns end().

Summary of Key Concepts:

- **Containers**: STL provides several container types like `vector`, `list`, `map`, and `set` to store data in different formats. Each container has its strengths, and understanding when to use each one is crucial for writing efficient code.

- **Iterators**: Iterators provide a uniform way to access elements in containers. They abstract away the details of how the container is implemented.

- **Algorithms**: STL provides a set of powerful algorithms that can be applied to containers using iterators. These algorithms make common tasks like sorting, searching, and modifying elements straightforward.

By mastering STL, you can leverage highly optimized and generic code to work with data structures and algorithms more efficiently. Let me know if you'd like more examples or need clarification on any part of the STL!

CHAPTER 6

ARRAYS AND MULTI-DIMENSIONAL ARRAYS

In this chapter, we'll explore **arrays** and **multi-dimensional arrays** in C++, which are fundamental data structures that allow you to store and manipulate collections of elements efficiently. Arrays are one of the simplest data structures but provide powerful capabilities for storing sequential data. Multi-dimensional arrays are used when you need to represent data in a grid or table-like structure.

Basic Array Operations

An **array** is a collection of elements of the same data type, stored in contiguous memory locations. In C++, arrays are fixed-size, meaning the size must be known at compile time.

Declaring and Initializing Arrays

To declare an array, you need to specify the type of its elements and the number of elements it will contain.

Syntax:

cpp

```
type arrayName[size];
```

- **type**: The data type of the elements (e.g., int, float).
- **arrayName**: The name you give to the array.
- **size**: The number of elements the array can hold.

Example:

cpp

```cpp
#include <iostream>
using namespace std;

int main() {
    int numbers[5] = {1, 2, 3, 4, 5};   // Declaring and initializing an array

    // Accessing array elements using indices
    cout << "First element: " << numbers[0] << endl;  // Output: 1
    cout << "Last element: " << numbers[4] << endl;   // Output: 5

    return 0;
}
```

Array Indexing

Arrays in C++ use **zero-based indexing**, meaning the first element is accessed at index 0, the second at index 1, and so on.

Example of accessing and modifying elements:

cpp

```cpp
#include <iostream>
using namespace std;

int main() {
    int arr[3] = {10, 20, 30};

    // Accessing elements
    cout << "Element at index 0: " << arr[0] <<
endl;  // Output: 10
    cout << "Element at index 1: " << arr[1] <<
endl;  // Output: 20
    cout << "Element at index 2: " << arr[2] <<
endl;  // Output: 30

    // Modifying an element
    arr[1] = 100;  // Changing value at index 1
    cout << "Modified element at index 1: " <<
arr[1] << endl;  // Output: 100

    return 0;
```

}

Array Size

In C++, the size of a statically declared array is fixed at compile time, and you can determine the size using the `sizeof` operator.

Example:

cpp

```
#include <iostream>
using namespace std;

int main() {
    int arr[10];
    cout << "Size of array: " << sizeof(arr) / sizeof(arr[0]) << endl;   // Output: 10
    return 0;
}
```

Here, `sizeof(arr)` gives the total size of the array in bytes, and `sizeof(arr[0])` gives the size of one element in the array. Dividing these gives the number of elements in the array.

Storing Data in Multi-Dimensional Arrays

A **multi-dimensional array** is essentially an array of arrays. These arrays can represent data structures such as matrices, tables, or grids. Multi-dimensional arrays are particularly useful for tasks

66

like image processing, scientific computing, and game development.

Declaring Multi-Dimensional Arrays

A two-dimensional array can be thought of as a table (rows and columns), while a three-dimensional array can be viewed as a cube or grid.

Syntax:

cpp

```cpp
type arrayName[rows][columns];  // 2D array
```

Example of a two-dimensional array:

cpp

```cpp
#include <iostream>
using namespace std;

int main() {
    // Declare a 2D array (3 rows and 4 columns)
    int matrix[3][4] = {
        {1, 2, 3, 4},
        {5, 6, 7, 8},
        {9, 10, 11, 12}
    };
```

```
    // Accessing elements in the 2D array
    cout << "Element at matrix[0][0]: " <<
matrix[0][0] << endl;  // Output: 1
    cout << "Element at matrix[1][2]: " <<
matrix[1][2] << endl;  // Output: 7
    cout << "Element at matrix[2][3]: " <<
matrix[2][3] << endl;  // Output: 12

    return 0;
}
```

Accessing and Modifying Multi-Dimensional Array Elements

You can access or modify elements in multi-dimensional arrays by specifying the index for each dimension.

Example:

cpp

```
#include <iostream>
using namespace std;

int main() {
    int matrix[2][3] = {{1, 2, 3}, {4, 5, 6}};

    // Modifying an element
    matrix[0][2] = 100;  // Changing element at
first row, third column
```

```cpp
    cout << "Modified matrix[0][2]: " <<
matrix[0][2] << endl;  // Output: 100

    return 0;
}
```

Initializing Multi-Dimensional Arrays

Arrays can be initialized during declaration, or you can initialize each element individually.

Example of initialization:

cpp

```cpp
int matrix[2][2] = {{1, 2}, {3, 4}};  // 2x2 matrix
```

If you don't initialize all elements, the remaining elements will default to 0.

Example of partial initialization:

cpp

```cpp
int matrix[3][3] = {{1, 2}, {3}};  // The remaining elements are initialized to 0
```

Real-World Examples of Arrays

Arrays are commonly used in a wide variety of real-world applications, especially where data can be organized in a list or grid. Here are a few examples of how arrays can be used:

Example 1: Storing Student Grades

Imagine you need to store the grades of 5 students in a class.

cpp

```cpp
#include <iostream>
using namespace std;

int main() {
    int grades[5] = {85, 90, 78, 92, 88};   // Grades of 5 students

    cout << "Student grades: ";
    for (int i = 0; i < 5; i++) {
        cout << grades[i] << " ";   // Output: 85 90 78 92 88
    }
    cout << endl;

    return 0;
}
```

70

Example 2: Representing a Game Grid (2D Array)

In a simple game like Tic-Tac-Toe, you might use a 3x3 array to represent the game board.

cpp

```
#include <iostream>
using namespace std;

int main() {
    char board[3][3] = {
        {'X', 'O', 'X'},
        {'O', 'X', 'O'},
        {'X', 'O', 'X'}
    };

    // Printing the board
    for (int i = 0; i < 3; i++) {
        for (int j = 0; j < 3; j++) {
            cout << board[i][j] << " ";
        }
        cout << endl;
    }

    return 0;
}
```

Example 3: Image Processing (Grayscale Image)

A grayscale image can be represented as a 2D array, where each element represents the pixel value.

cpp

```cpp
#include <iostream>
using namespace std;

int main() {
    int image[4][4] = {
        {255, 0, 255, 0},
        {255, 255, 0, 255},
        {0, 0, 0, 255},
        {255, 255, 255, 255}
    };

    // Print the image data
    for (int i = 0; i < 4; i++) {
        for (int j = 0; j < 4; j++) {
            cout << image[i][j] << " ";    // 
Output: Pixel values
        }
        cout << endl;
    }

    return 0;
}
```

In this example, the 2D array could represent a 4x4 pixel image, where each value is the grayscale intensity of a pixel.

Summary of Key Concepts:

- **Arrays**: Arrays are collections of elements of the same data type, stored in contiguous memory locations. They provide efficient access to elements via indices.
- **Multi-Dimensional Arrays**: Arrays with more than one dimension (e.g., 2D arrays for matrices) are useful for representing data in grid-like structures.
- **Real-World Examples**: Arrays are widely used in various real-world applications such as storing student grades, representing game boards, and handling image data.

Arrays are essential building blocks for many data structures and algorithms, and mastering their use will help you handle a wide variety of data-related problems efficiently. Let me know if you need further examples or clarifications!

CHAPTER 7

LINKED LISTS: SINGLY AND DOUBLY

In this chapter, we'll explore **linked lists**, one of the most important dynamic data structures in computer science. Unlike arrays, linked lists allow for efficient insertions and deletions without needing to shift elements, making them useful for dynamic data storage. We'll cover both **singly linked lists** and **doubly linked lists**, their operations, and some real-world applications.

Introduction to Linked Lists

A **linked list** is a linear collection of elements where each element is stored in a **node**, and each node contains two parts:

- **Data**: The value stored in the node.
- **Next (or Pointer)**: A reference (or pointer) to the next node in the sequence.

In a **singly linked list**, each node points to the next node in the list, while the last node points to `nullptr` (indicating the end of the list).

In a **doubly linked list**, each node has two pointers: one pointing to the next node and another pointing to the previous node.

Singly Linked List Structure

In a singly linked list, each node contains:

1. **Data**: The actual information stored.
2. **Next**: A pointer to the next node in the list.

Visual Representation:

css

```
[Data | Next] -> [Data | Next] -> [Data | Next]
-> nullptr
```

Doubly Linked List Structure

In a doubly linked list, each node contains:

1. **Data**: The actual information stored.
2. **Next**: A pointer to the next node in the list.
3. **Prev**: A pointer to the previous node in the list.

Visual Representation:

css

```
nullptr <- [Prev | Data | Next] <-> [Prev | Data
| Next] <-> [Prev | Data | Next] -> nullptr
```

Operations: Insertion, Deletion, Traversal

We will now discuss the main operations that can be performed on linked lists: **insertion, deletion**, and **traversal**.

Insertion in Linked Lists

Insertion involves adding a new node into the list. The insertion can be done at various positions in the list, such as at the **beginning, end**, or **in the middle**.

- **Insertion at the Beginning**: The new node becomes the new head of the list.
- **Insertion at the End**: The new node is added after the last node.
- **Insertion in the Middle**: The new node is added between two existing nodes.

Example: Insertion at the Beginning (Singly Linked List)

cpp

```cpp
#include <iostream>
using namespace std;

class Node {
public:
```

```cpp
    int data;
    Node* next;

    Node(int value) {
        data = value;
        next = nullptr;
    }
};

class LinkedList {
public:
    Node* head;

    LinkedList() {
        head = nullptr;
    }

    // Insertion at the beginning
    void insertAtBeginning(int value) {
        Node* newNode = new Node(value);
        newNode->next = head;   // Point the new
node's next to the current head
        head = newNode;           // Make the new
node the head of the list
    }

    // Traverse the list and print elements
    void traverse() {
        Node* temp = head;
```

```
        while (temp != nullptr) {
            cout << temp->data << " ";
            temp = temp->next;
        }
        cout << endl;
    }
};

int main() {
    LinkedList list;
    list.insertAtBeginning(10);
    list.insertAtBeginning(20);
    list.insertAtBeginning(30);

    list.traverse();   // Output: 30 20 10
    return 0;
}
```

Deletion in Linked Lists

Deletion involves removing a node from the list. The node can be deleted from the **beginning**, **end**, or **middle**.

- **Deletion at the Beginning**: The head is updated to point to the next node.
- **Deletion at the End**: Traverse the list to find the second-to-last node, update its `next` pointer to `nullptr`, and delete the last node.

- **Deletion in the Middle**: The `next` pointer of the node before the one being deleted is updated to skip the node being removed.

Example: Deletion at the Beginning (Singly Linked List)

cpp

```cpp
#include <iostream>
using namespace std;

class Node {
public:
    int data;
    Node* next;

    Node(int value) {
        data = value;
        next = nullptr;
    }
};

class LinkedList {
public:
    Node* head;

    LinkedList() {
        head = nullptr;
    }
```

```cpp
    // Deletion at the beginning
    void deleteAtBeginning() {
        if (head != nullptr) {
            Node* temp = head;
            head = head->next;   // Move head to
the next node
            delete temp;         // Free memory of
the old head
        }
    }

    // Traverse the list and print elements
    void traverse() {
        Node* temp = head;
        while (temp != nullptr) {
            cout << temp->data << " ";
            temp = temp->next;
        }
        cout << endl;
    }
};

int main() {
    LinkedList list;
    list.insertAtBeginning(10);
    list.insertAtBeginning(20);
    list.insertAtBeginning(30);
```

```cpp
list.traverse();   // Output: 30 20 10

list.deleteAtBeginning();
list.traverse();   // Output: 20 10

return 0;
}
```

Traversal in Linked Lists

Traversal means going through each element of the linked list from the head to the end. This is a common operation used in insertion, deletion, and searching.

Example: Traversal in a Singly Linked List

cpp

```cpp
#include <iostream>
using namespace std;

class Node {
public:
    int data;
    Node* next;

    Node(int value) {
        data = value;
        next = nullptr;
    }
```

```cpp
};

class LinkedList {
public:
    Node* head;

    LinkedList() {
        head = nullptr;
    }

    // Insertion at the beginning
    void insertAtBeginning(int value) {
        Node* newNode = new Node(value);
        newNode->next = head;
        head = newNode;
    }

    // Traverse the list and print elements
    void traverse() {
        Node* temp = head;
        while (temp != nullptr) {
            cout << temp->data << " ";
            temp = temp->next;
        }
        cout << endl;
    }
};

int main() {
```

```
LinkedList list;
list.insertAtBeginning(10);
list.insertAtBeginning(20);
list.insertAtBeginning(30);

list.traverse();   // Output: 30 20 10

return 0;
}
```

Applications and Use Cases of Linked Lists

Linked lists are widely used in various applications due to their flexibility and efficiency in certain scenarios. Some common applications include:

1. Implementing Data Structures

- **Stacks and Queues**: Linked lists are commonly used to implement stacks and queues, where elements need to be added or removed from either end of the list efficiently.
- **Dynamic Memory Allocation**: Linked lists allow memory to be allocated dynamically as needed, making them ideal for situations where the size of the data structure is unknown or changes frequently.

2. Memory Management

- **Free List Management**: In dynamic memory allocation (e.g., managing heap memory), linked lists can be used to manage the blocks of free memory.

3. Real-Time Systems

- **Task Scheduling**: In real-time systems, linked lists can be used to manage tasks in a queue that need to be processed in a certain order. The insertion and deletion operations are performed efficiently without the need for shifting data.

4. Undo/Redo Operations

- **Undo/Redo Stack**: Linked lists can be used to implement undo and redo operations, where each operation is saved as a node, and traversing the list allows you to move backward or forward through the actions.

5. Graph Representation

- **Adjacency List for Graphs**: Linked lists are often used to represent graphs, where each vertex is connected to other vertices through edges stored in a linked list format. This allows efficient traversal and manipulation of graph data.

Summary of Key Concepts:

- **Singly Linked List**: A list where each node contains data and a pointer to the next node. It is efficient for insertions and deletions at the beginning and allows sequential access to elements.

- **Doubly Linked List**: A more advanced linked list where each node contains a pointer to both the next and previous nodes, allowing bidirectional traversal.

- **Linked List Operations**: Include insertion, deletion, and traversal. These operations are efficient when it comes to adding and removing elements without shifting data.

- **Applications**: Linked lists are used in various applications such as implementing dynamic data structures, task scheduling, memory management, and graph representation.

Understanding linked lists will help you work with dynamic data structures and optimize memory usage. Let me know if you'd like more examples or further explanation on any topic!

CHAPTER 8

STACKS AND QUEUES

In this chapter, we will explore **stacks** and **queues**, which are fundamental data structures in computer science. Both of these structures are linear, but they differ in how elements are inserted and removed. We will cover the basics of each, including their operations and implementations, as well as their real-world applications.

Understanding the Stack Data Structure

A **stack** is a collection of elements that follows the **Last In, First Out (LIFO)** principle. This means that the last element added to the stack is the first one to be removed. Think of it like a stack of plates — you add plates to the top, and you remove plates from the top.

Basic Stack Operations

1. **Push**: Adds an element to the top of the stack.
2. **Pop**: Removes the top element from the stack.
3. **Peek (or Top)**: Returns the top element without removing it.
4. **isEmpty**: Checks whether the stack is empty.

Visual Representation:

kotlin

```
|   |        <- Top (pop removes this element)
| 3 |
| 2 |
| 1 |        <- Bottom
```

Stack Implementation (using an array)

A stack can be implemented using an array or a linked list. Let's implement a stack using a dynamic array.

cpp

```cpp
#include <iostream>
#include <vector>
using namespace std;

class Stack {
private:
    vector<int> stack;

public:
    // Push an element to the stack
    void push(int value) {
        stack.push_back(value);
    }
```

```
    // Pop an element from the stack
    void pop() {
        if (!isEmpty()) {
            stack.pop_back();  // Remove the last
element
        }
    }


    // Peek the top element
    int peek() {
        if (!isEmpty()) {
            return stack.back();
        }
        return -1;  // Return -1 if the stack is
empty
    }


    // Check if the stack is empty
    bool isEmpty() {
        return stack.empty();
    }


    // Display the stack
    void display() {
        for (int i = stack.size() - 1; i >= 0; -
-i) {
            cout << stack[i] << " ";
        }
        cout << endl;
```

```
    }
};

int main() {
    Stack s;
    s.push(10);
    s.push(20);
    s.push(30);

    cout << "Stack contents: ";
    s.display();   // Output: 30 20 10

    cout << "Top element: " << s.peek() << endl;
// Output: 30

    s.pop();
    cout << "Stack after pop: ";
    s.display();   // Output: 20 10

    return 0;
}
```

In this example:

- **Push** adds an element to the stack.
- **Pop** removes the top element from the stack.
- **Peek** returns the top element without removing it.

Implementing Queues: Basic and Circular

A **queue** is a collection of elements that follows the **First In, First Out (FIFO)** principle. This means that the first element added to the queue is the first one to be removed. You can think of it as a line at a ticket counter — the first person to arrive is the first one to be served.

Basic Queue Operations

1. **Enqueue**: Adds an element to the rear of the queue.
2. **Dequeue**: Removes an element from the front of the queue.
3. **Front**: Returns the element at the front without removing it.
4. **isEmpty**: Checks whether the queue is empty.
5. **Size**: Returns the number of elements in the queue.

Visual Representation of a Queue:

```rust
```

```
Front -> | 1 | 2 | 3 | 4 | <- Rear
```

Queue Implementation (using an array)

A basic queue can be implemented using an array or a linked list. Let's implement a queue using an array.

cpp

```cpp
#include <iostream>
using namespace std;

class Queue {
private:
    int front, rear, size;
    int* queue;

public:
    Queue(int s) {
        size = s;
        front = -1;
        rear = -1;
        queue = new int[size];
    }

    // Enqueue an element
    void enqueue(int value) {
        if (rear == size - 1) {
            cout << "Queue is full." << endl;
        } else {
            if (front == -1) front = 0;   // If
queue is empty, set front to 0
            queue[++rear] = value;   // Insert
element at the rear
        }
    }
```

```cpp
// Dequeue an element
void dequeue() {
    if (front == -1 || front > rear) {
        cout << "Queue is empty." << endl;
    } else {
        front++;  // Remove the front element
    }
}

// Get the front element
int frontElement() {
    if (front == -1 || front > rear) {
        return -1;  // Return -1 if the queue
is empty
    }
    return queue[front];
}

// Check if the queue is empty
bool isEmpty() {
    return (front == -1 || front > rear);
}

// Display the queue
void display() {
    if (front == -1 || front > rear) {
        cout << "Queue is empty." << endl;
    } else {
```

```cpp
        for (int i = front; i <= rear; ++i)
{

            cout << queue[i] << " ";
        }
        cout << endl;
    }
    }
};

int main() {
    Queue q(5);

    q.enqueue(10);
    q.enqueue(20);
    q.enqueue(30);
    q.enqueue(40);

    cout << "Queue contents: ";
    q.display();  // Output: 10 20 30 40

    q.dequeue();
    cout << "Queue after dequeue: ";
    q.display();  // Output: 20 30 40

    cout << "Front element: " << q.frontElement()
<< endl;  // Output: 20

    return 0;
}
```

In this example:

- **Enqueue** adds an element to the queue.
- **Dequeue** removes the front element from the queue.
- **Front** returns the front element without removing it.

Circular Queue

A **circular queue** is a variation of the regular queue where the rear end connects to the front end, forming a circle. This helps to efficiently use the available space in a fixed-size queue.

In a regular queue, when elements are dequeued, the front index moves forward, leaving gaps in the array. In a circular queue, when the front or rear reaches the end of the array, it wraps around to the beginning, reusing the empty space.

Circular Queue Operations:

1. **Enqueue**: Adds an element to the rear. If the rear is at the end, it wraps around.
2. **Dequeue**: Removes an element from the front.
3. **Front**: Returns the front element.
4. **Rear**: Returns the rear element.

Visual Representation of a Circular Queue:

```
nginx
```

```
Front -> | 1 | 2 | 3 | 4 | <- Rear
           ^                 ^
           |                 |
         ---- Wraps Around ---
```

Real-World Applications of Stacks and Queues

Stacks and **queues** have various real-world applications:

Real-World Applications of Stacks:

1. **Undo/Redo Operations**: Stacks are used in applications like text editors where the most recent action can be undone or redone.
2. **Expression Evaluation**: In compilers or calculators, stacks are used for evaluating expressions (e.g., infix, postfix, or prefix).
3. **Function Calls (Call Stack)**: The operating system uses a stack to manage function calls and recursion. When a function is called, its execution context is pushed onto the stack, and when it returns, the context is popped off.

Real-World Applications of Queues:

1. **Task Scheduling**: In operating systems, queues are used to manage processes. The first task that arrives is the first one to be processed.

2. **Customer Service Systems**: Queues are used to manage customers in line for service (e.g., call centers, checkout lines).

3. **Breadth-First Search (BFS)**: In graph traversal algorithms, BFS uses a queue to explore nodes level by level.

Summary of Key Concepts:

- **Stacks** follow the LIFO (Last In, First Out) principle and support operations like **push, pop, peek**, and **isEmpty**.
- **Queues** follow the FIFO (First In, First Out) principle and support operations like **enqueue, dequeue, front**, and **isEmpty**.
- **Circular Queues** help optimize space by reusing the empty areas in a fixed-size queue.
- Real-world applications of **stacks** and **queues** include undo operations, task scheduling, and graph traversal.

Understanding stacks and queues will help you solve problems that require efficient management of data in a linear fashion. Let me know if you need further explanations or more examples!

CHAPTER 9

HASH TABLES AND HASH MAPS

In this chapter, we will dive into **hash tables** and **hash maps**, which are crucial data structures used to store and retrieve data efficiently. Hash tables are widely used in scenarios where fast access to data is required, such as in databases, caches, and dictionaries. We will explore the concept of **hashing**, **collision resolution techniques**, and how to use **hash maps** in C++.

Introduction to Hashing

Hashing is a technique used to uniquely identify a data element by converting it into a fixed-size value, called a **hash code** or **hash value**. A **hash function** is used to generate this hash value based on the input data. The hash value determines the index in the hash table where the corresponding value will be stored.

In a **hash table**, data is stored in an array-like structure, but instead of using numeric indices, the index is computed using the hash value of the key.

Key Concept:

- **Hash Function**: A function that takes a key and returns an index (or hash value). A good hash function distributes keys uniformly across the table to minimize collisions.

Hash Table Structure

A **hash table** consists of:

1. **Array**: The underlying data structure where the values are stored.
2. **Hash Function**: A function that maps the key to an index in the array.
3. **Buckets/Slots**: Each slot or bucket in the array holds a key-value pair.

Example:

css

```
Index 0 -> [key1, value1]
Index 1 -> [key2, value2]
Index 2 -> [key3, value3]
```

Collision Resolution Techniques

Collisions occur when two different keys hash to the same index in the hash table. Since a hash table is an array, each index can only hold one element. Thus, we need techniques to resolve collisions.

1. Chaining (Separate Chaining)

In **chaining**, each bucket in the hash table contains a linked list (or another collection) of key-value pairs. If multiple keys hash to the same index, they are stored in the linked list at that index.

Example:

css

```
Index 0 -> [(key1, value1), (key4, value4)]
Index 1 -> [(key2, value2)]
Index 2 -> [(key3, value3), (key5, value5)]
```

2. Open Addressing (Probing)

In **open addressing**, when a collision occurs, we look for the next available slot in the table based on a specific probing technique. The most common probing techniques are:

- **Linear Probing**: If a collision occurs, check the next slot (index + 1), and continue checking until an empty slot is found.
- **Quadratic Probing**: If a collision occurs, check the next slot based on a quadratic function (index + 1^2, index + 2^2, etc.).
- **Double Hashing**: Use a second hash function to calculate the step size when a collision occurs.

Using Hash Maps in C++

In C++, the **Standard Template Library (STL)** provides a built-in hash map implementation called `unordered_map`. It is an associative container that uses hashing to store key-value pairs, providing average constant-time complexity (O(1)) for insertions, deletions, and lookups.

Basic Operations in `unordered_map`

1. **Insert**: Adds a key-value pair to the map.
2. **Find**: Searches for a key and returns an iterator to the corresponding value.
3. **Erase**: Removes a key-value pair from the map.
4. **Access**: Retrieves the value associated with a key.

Example: Using `unordered_map` in C++

cpp

```
#include <iostream>
#include <unordered_map>
using namespace std;

int main() {
    // Create an unordered_map (hash map)
    unordered_map<string, int> studentGrades;

    // Insert key-value pairs
```

```cpp
studentGrades["Alice"] = 90;
studentGrades["Bob"] = 85;
studentGrades["Charlie"] = 92;

// Accessing values by key
cout << "Alice's grade: " << studentGrades["Alice"] << endl;  // Output: 90

// Checking if a key exists
if (studentGrades.find("Bob") != studentGrades.end()) {
    cout << "Bob's grade: " << studentGrades["Bob"] << endl;  // Output: 85
} else {
    cout << "Bob not found." << endl;
}

// Erasing a key-value pair
studentGrades.erase("Charlie");

// Traversing and printing all key-value pairs
cout << "Remaining student grades:" << endl;
for (const auto& pair : studentGrades) {
    cout << pair.first << ": " << pair.second << endl;
}
// Output:
// Alice: 90
```

```
// Bob: 85

return 0;
}
```

In this example:

- **Insert**: Adds key-value pairs (e.g., `Alice -> 90`).
- **Access**: Retrieves the value associated with a key (e.g., `studentGrades["Alice"]`).
- **Find**: Searches for a key to check if it exists in the map.
- **Erase**: Removes a key-value pair from the map.

Advantages of `unordered_map` in C++

- Provides **constant time complexity** (O(1)) for average-case insertions, deletions, and lookups.
- The keys in an `unordered_map` are stored in **no particular order**, as the underlying implementation uses hashing.

Custom Hash Functions

By default, `unordered_map` uses the `std::hash` function for hashing, but you can define your own custom hash function if needed.

Example: Custom hash function for a custom type (e.g., a Person class)

cpp

```cpp
#include <iostream>
#include <unordered_map>
using namespace std;

class Person {
public:
    string name;
    int age;

    Person(string n, int a) : name(n), age(a) {}
};

// Custom hash function for Person
struct PersonHash {
    size_t operator()(const Person& p) const {
        return      hash<string>()(p.name)      ^
hash<int>()(p.age);
    }
};

int main() {
    unordered_map<Person,   string,   PersonHash>
personMap;
```

```cpp
    // Create Person objects
    Person p1("Alice", 30);
    Person p2("Bob", 25);

    // Insert custom objects into the
unordered_map
    personMap[p1] = "Engineer";
    personMap[p2] = "Doctor";

    // Accessing values by key
    cout << "Alice's job: " << personMap[p1] <<
endl;  // Output: Engineer
    cout << "Bob's job: " << personMap[p2] <<
endl;    // Output: Doctor

    return 0;
}
```

In this example, a custom hash function is created for the `Person` class, which uses both the `name` and `age` attributes to generate a hash value.

Summary of Key Concepts:

- **Hashing**: A technique for mapping keys to indices in a hash table using a hash function. It enables efficient searching, insertion, and deletion in constant time, on average.

- **Hash Tables**: A data structure that stores key-value pairs, using a hash function to compute the index where the value is stored. Collisions are handled using techniques such as chaining or open addressing.

- **Collision Resolution**: When two keys hash to the same index, we need methods like **chaining** (linked lists) or **open addressing** (probing) to resolve collisions.

- **Hash Maps**: In C++, `unordered_map` is a hash map implementation that provides fast average-case lookups and insertions. It can be customized with a user-defined hash function.

Hash tables and hash maps are essential for solving problems that involve fast lookups and efficient data storage. They are commonly used in databases, caches, and associative containers like dictionaries.

CHAPTER 10

TREES: BASICS AND BINARY TREES

In this chapter, we will cover **trees** and **binary trees**, which are hierarchical data structures that are commonly used in a variety of applications such as database indexing, network routing, and file systems. We will explore the fundamentals of trees, the structure and operations of binary trees, and various **tree traversal techniques**.

Introduction to Trees

A **tree** is a non-linear data structure consisting of nodes connected by edges. It is used to represent hierarchical relationships where there is a root node, and each node may have child nodes.

Key terms:

- **Node**: An element in the tree that contains data.
- **Root**: The topmost node in the tree. It has no parent.
- **Parent**: A node that has one or more child nodes.
- **Child**: A node that is a descendant of another node.
- **Leaf**: A node that has no children.
- **Subtree**: A tree formed by a node and its descendants.

- **Depth**: The level of a node in the tree. The root node has a depth of 0.
- **Height**: The longest path from a node to a leaf node.

Visual Representation of a Tree:

mathematica

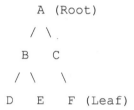

```
    A (Root)
   / \
  B   C
 / \   \
D   E   F (Leaf)
```

In this example:

- A is the root.
- B and C are children of A.
- D, E, and F are leaf nodes.

Binary Trees and Binary Search Trees

Binary Trees

A **binary tree** is a special type of tree where each node can have at most two children: a **left child** and a **right child**.

Characteristics of Binary Trees:

1. Each node has a maximum of two children.

2. The children are referred to as the **left** and **right** children.

3. The left child always appears before the right child.

Example of a Binary Tree:

markdown

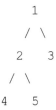

```
        1
       / \
      2   3
     / \
    4   5
```

In this example, node 1 is the root, 2 and 3 are the children of node 1, 4 and 5 are the children of node 2.

Binary Search Trees (BST)

A **binary search tree (BST)** is a type of binary tree that maintains a specific order property:

- For every node in the tree:
    - The **left child** has a value less than the node's value.
    - The **right child** has a value greater than the node's value.

This property allows for efficient searching, insertion, and deletion.

Example of a Binary Search Tree:


```
        8
      /   \
     3    10
    / \     \
   1   6    14
      / \   /
     4   7 13
```

In this example:

- The root node is 8. The left subtree contains nodes with values less than 8, and the right subtree contains nodes with values greater than 8.
- This ordering ensures that searching for a value in the tree is efficient (O(log n) time complexity, on average).

Tree Traversal Techniques (In-order, Pre-order, Post-order)

Tree traversal refers to the process of visiting all the nodes in a tree in a specific order. The three most common types of depth-first traversals are:

- **In-order traversal**
- **Pre-order traversal**
- **Post-order traversal**

1. In-order Traversal

In **in-order traversal**, the nodes are visited in the following order:

1. Visit the left subtree.
2. Visit the node.
3. Visit the right subtree.

In-order traversal of a Binary Search Tree (BST) will result in visiting the nodes in ascending order of their values.

Example:

sql

```
In-order traversal of the tree:
        8
       / \
      3    10
     / \     \
    1   6     14
       / \    /
      4   7  13


Result: 1, 3, 4, 6, 7, 8, 10, 13, 14
```

C++ Code for In-order Traversal:

cpp

110

```cpp
#include <iostream>
using namespace std;

class Node {
public:
    int data;
    Node* left;
    Node* right;

    Node(int val) {
        data = val;
        left = nullptr;
        right = nullptr;
    }
};

void inOrderTraversal(Node* root) {
    if (root != nullptr) {
        inOrderTraversal(root->left);    // Visit left subtree
        cout << root->data << " ";       // Visit node
        inOrderTraversal(root->right);   // Visit right subtree
    }
}

int main() {
    Node* root = new Node(8);
```

```
root->left = new Node(3);
root->right = new Node(10);
root->left->left = new Node(1);
root->left->right = new Node(6);
root->left->right->left = new Node(4);
root->left->right->right = new Node(7);
root->right->right = new Node(14);
root->right->right->left = new Node(13);

cout << "In-order Traversal: ";
inOrderTraversal(root);   // Output: 1 3 4 6
7 8 10 13 14
cout << endl;

return 0;
}
```

2. Pre-order Traversal

In **pre-order traversal**, the nodes are visited in the following order:

1. Visit the node.
2. Visit the left subtree.
3. Visit the right subtree.

Pre-order traversal of the tree:

```
makefile
```

```
        8
      /  \
     3    10
   /  \      \
  1    6   .  14
     /  \   /
    4    7 13
```

Result: 8, 3, 1, 6, 4, 7, 10, 14, 13

C++ Code for Pre-order Traversal:

cpp

```cpp
void preOrderTraversal(Node* root) {
    if (root != nullptr) {
        cout << root->data << " ";      // Visit
node
        preOrderTraversal(root->left); // Visit
left subtree
        preOrderTraversal(root->right); // Visit
right subtree
    }
}

cout << "Pre-order Traversal: ";
preOrderTraversal(root);  // Output: 8 3 1 6 4 7
10 14 13
cout << endl;
```

3. Post-order Traversal

In **post-order traversal**, the nodes are visited in the following order:

1. Visit the left subtree.
2. Visit the right subtree.
3. Visit the node.

Post-order traversal of the tree:

makefile

```
        8
       / \
      3    10
     / \     \
    1   6    14
       / \   /
      4   7 13
```

Result: 1, 4, 7, 6, 3, 13, 14, 10, 8

C++ Code for Post-order Traversal:

cpp

```
void postOrderTraversal(Node* root) {
    if (root != nullptr) {
```

114

```
        postOrderTraversal(root->left);        //
Visit left subtree
        postOrderTraversal(root->right);       //
Visit right subtree
        cout << root->data << " ";        // Visit
node
    }
}
```

```
cout << "Post-order Traversal: ";
postOrderTraversal(root);   // Output: 1 4 7 6 3
13 14 10 8
cout << endl;
```

Summary of Key Concepts:

- **Binary Trees**: A tree where each node has at most two children, called left and right.

- **Binary Search Trees (BST)**: A binary tree where the left child is smaller than the parent node, and the right child is larger. This structure allows for efficient searching, insertion, and deletion.

- **Tree Traversals**: Methods to visit all nodes in a tree:
    - **In-order**: Left, Root, Right (for BST, this gives ascending order).
    - **Pre-order**: Root, Left, Right.
    - **Post-order**: Left, Right, Root.

Binary trees and binary search trees are foundational for various algorithms and are commonly used in databases, searching algorithms, and decision-making processes. Understanding these trees and traversal methods is essential for building efficient software. Let me know if you'd like more examples or further explanations!

CHAPTER 11

HEAPS AND PRIORITY QUEUES

In this chapter, we will explore **heaps** and **priority queues**, which are specialized tree-based data structures used to manage elements with priority. Heaps are used in many applications such as sorting algorithms (like heapsort), task scheduling, and implementing efficient priority queues.

Introduction to Heaps

A **heap** is a complete binary tree where each node satisfies a specific **heap property**:

- **Max-Heap**: For any given node i, the value of i is greater than or equal to the values of its children.
- **Min-Heap**: For any given node i, the value of i is less than or equal to the values of its children.

Heaps are typically implemented as binary trees, but they can also be efficiently stored in arrays. They are mainly used for **priority queues**, sorting, and algorithms that need to repeatedly access the largest or smallest element.

Max-Heap vs Min-Heap

- **Max-Heap**: The root node has the largest value in the heap. In a max-heap, the parent node is always greater than or equal to its children.

- **Min-Heap**: The root node has the smallest value in the heap. In a min-heap, the parent node is always less than or equal to its children.

Visual Representation:

Max-Heap:

markdown

```
      10
     /  \
    5    3
   / \  / \
  2  4 1  0
```

Min-Heap:

markdown

```
      1
     / \
    3   5
   / \ / \
```

6   7   8   9

Heap Operations

The primary operations that can be performed on a heap are:

1. **Insert**: Add an element to the heap and ensure the heap property is maintained.

2. **Extract-Max/Extract-Min**: Remove and return the root element (either the maximum in a max-heap or the minimum in a min-heap) and maintain the heap property.

3. **Heapify**: Adjust the heap to restore the heap property after an insertion or deletion.

Implementing Heaps

Heaps are usually implemented using an array for efficient storage:

- The root node is at index 0.
- For any node at index i, the left child is at index 2*i + 1 and the right child is at index 2*i + 2.
- The parent of any node at index i is at index (i - 1) / 2.

Max-Heap Implementation

Let's look at a basic implementation of a max-heap.

C++ Code for Max-Heap:

cpp

```cpp
#include <iostream>
#include <vector>
using namespace std;

class MaxHeap {
private:
    vector<int> heap;

    // Helper function to heapify a subtree
rooted at index i
    void heapify(int i) {
        int largest = i;
        int left = 2 * i + 1;
        int right = 2 * i + 2;

        if (left < heap.size() && heap[left] >
heap[largest])
            largest = left;
        if (right < heap.size() && heap[right] >
heap[largest])
            largest = right;

        if (largest != i) {
            swap(heap[i], heap[largest]);
            heapify(largest);    // Recursively
heapify the affected subtree
```

```
        }
    }


public:
    // Insert a new element into the heap
    void insert(int val) {
        heap.push_back(val);
        int i = heap.size() - 1;


        // Maintain heap property by bubbling up
the new element
        while (i > 0 && heap[(i - 1) / 2] <
heap[i]) {
            swap(heap[i], heap[(i - 1) / 2]);
            i = (i - 1) / 2;
        }
    }


    // Extract the maximum element from the heap
    int extractMax() {
        if (heap.size() == 0) return -1;    //
Empty heap
        if (heap.size() == 1) {
            int max = heap[0];
            heap.pop_back();
            return max;
        }


    // Swap the root with the last element
```

```cpp
        int max = heap[0];
        heap[0] = heap[heap.size() - 1];
        heap.pop_back();

        heapify(0);  // Restore the heap property
        return max;
    }


    // Display the heap
    void display() {
        for (int val : heap) {
            cout << val << " ";
        }
        cout << endl;
    }
};


int main() {
    MaxHeap maxHeap;

    // Insert elements into the heap
    maxHeap.insert(10);
    maxHeap.insert(20);
    maxHeap.insert(5);
    maxHeap.insert(30);
    maxHeap.insert(15);

    cout << "Max Heap: ";
    maxHeap.display();  // Output: 30 20 10 5 15
```

```cpp
    // Extract the maximum element
    cout << "Extracted max: " <<
maxHeap.extractMax() << endl;  // Output: 30

    cout << "Max Heap after extraction: ";
    maxHeap.display();  // Output: 20 15 10 5

    return 0;
}
```

Explanation:

- The `insert` function adds a new element to the heap, maintaining the heap property by **bubbling up** the element.
- The `extractMax` function removes the root of the heap (the maximum element) and restores the heap property by **heapifying** the tree.
- The `heapify` function ensures that the heap property is maintained after a change in the heap.

Min-Heap Implementation

A min-heap works similarly to a max-heap, but the heap property is reversed — the parent node must be less than or equal to its children.

C++ Code for Min-Heap:

```cpp
class MinHeap {
private:
    vector<int> heap;

    // Helper function to heapify a subtree
rooted at index i
    void heapify(int i) {
        int smallest = i;
        int left = 2 * i + 1;
        int right = 2 * i + 2;

        if (left < heap.size() && heap[left] <
heap[smallest])
            smallest = left;
        if (right < heap.size() && heap[right] <
heap[smallest])
            smallest = right;

        if (smallest != i) {
            swap(heap[i], heap[smallest]);
            heapify(smallest);    // Recursively
heapify the affected subtree
        }
    }

public:
    // Insert a new element into the heap
```

124

```cpp
void insert(int val) {
    heap.push_back(val);
    int i = heap.size() - 1;

    // Maintain heap property by bubbling up
the new element
    while (i > 0 && heap[(i - 1) / 2] >
heap[i]) {
        swap(heap[i], heap[(i - 1) / 2]);
        i = (i - 1) / 2;
    }
}


// Extract the minimum element from the heap
int extractMin() {
    if (heap.size() == 0) return -1;    //
Empty heap
    if (heap.size() == 1) {
        int min = heap[0];
        heap.pop_back();
        return min;
    }

    // Swap the root with the last element
    int min = heap[0];
    heap[0] = heap[heap.size() - 1];
    heap.pop_back();

    heapify(0);  // Restore the heap property
```

```
        return min;
    }


    // Display the heap
    void display() {
        for (int val : heap) {
            cout << val << " ";
        }
        cout << endl;
    }
};
```

The min-heap implementation works similarly to the max-heap but ensures the smallest element is always at the root.

Implementing Priority Queues

A **priority queue** is a data structure where each element is associated with a priority. Elements with higher priority are dequeued before elements with lower priority. Heaps are often used to implement priority queues because they allow for efficient extraction of the highest or lowest priority element.

Using a Priority Queue in C++ (STL)

C++ provides the `priority_queue` class in the **Standard Template Library (STL)** to easily implement priority queues. By default, it implements a max-heap.

Example of Using a Priority Queue in C++:

cpp

```cpp
#include <iostream>
#include <queue>
using namespace std;

int main() {
    // Create a max-heap priority queue
    priority_queue<int> pq;

    // Insert elements into the priority queue
    pq.push(10);
    pq.push(20);
    pq.push(5);
    pq.push(30);

    cout << "Priority Queue (Max-Heap): ";
    while (!pq.empty()) {
        cout << pq.top() << " ";  // Output the
largest element
        pq.pop();                 // Remove the
largest element
    }
    cout << endl;

    // Create a min-heap priority queue by using
a custom comparator
```

```
    priority_queue<int,                 vector<int>,
greater<int>> minPq;
    minPq.push(10);
    minPq.push(20);
    minPq.push(5);
    minPq.push(30);

    cout << "Priority Queue (Min-Heap): ";
    while (!minPq.empty()) {
        cout << minPq.top() << " ";    // Output
the smallest element
        minPq.pop();                    // Remove
the smallest element
    }
    cout << endl;

    return 0;
}
```

Explanation:

- The **default priority_queue** creates a max-heap, so elements with higher values have higher priority.
- To create a **min-heap**, we use the **greater<int>** comparator, which reverses the order and makes the smallest element have the highest priority.

Summary of Key Concepts:

- **Heaps**: A heap is a binary tree-based data structure that satisfies the heap property. In a **max-heap**, the parent node is greater than or equal to its children, while in a **min-heap**, the parent node is less than or equal to its children.

- **Priority Queue**: A data structure where elements are dequeued based on priority. Heaps are commonly used to implement priority queues.

- **Operations**: The main operations on heaps are **insert**, **extract (max/min)**, and **heapify**. These operations are efficient (O(log n) time complexity) due to the structure of the heap.

Heaps and priority queues are crucial for efficient algorithms like **Dijkstra's shortest path, Huffman encoding**, and **heap sort**. Let me know if you need more examples or further explanations!

CHAPTER 12

BALANCED TREES: AVL AND RED-BLACK TREES

In this chapter, we will explore **balanced trees**, specifically **AVL trees** and **Red-Black trees**, which are types of self-balancing binary search trees (BST). These trees maintain their balance automatically, ensuring that operations such as search, insertion, and deletion are efficient, with a time complexity of **O(log n)**.

Introduction to Balanced Trees

A **balanced tree** is a type of binary search tree (BST) where the height of the left and right subtrees of every node differs by at most a constant factor (usually 1). This balance ensures that the tree remains relatively shallow, which guarantees logarithmic time complexity for search, insertion, and deletion operations.

In an **unbalanced BST**, operations can degrade to **O(n)** if the tree becomes skewed (e.g., a tree that degenerates into a linked list). However, balanced trees avoid this issue by maintaining balance during insertion and deletion.

Two popular types of self-balancing BSTs are:

1. **AVL Trees**: These trees maintain a strict balance factor (the difference in height between left and right subtrees) of at most 1.

2. **Red-Black Trees**: These trees enforce a set of rules (colors and rotations) to keep the tree balanced during insertions and deletions.

AVL Trees

An **AVL tree** (named after its inventors Adelson-Velsky and Landis) is a self-balancing binary search tree where the balance factor of every node is between -1 and 1. The **balance factor** of a node is defined as:

- ```
  balance  factor  =  height(left  subtree)  -
  height(right subtree)
  ```

If a node's balance factor becomes less than -1 or greater than 1, the tree becomes unbalanced, and rotations are needed to restore balance.

AVL Tree Rotations

To restore balance, we use **rotations**. There are four types of rotations in AVL trees:

1. **Right Rotation (Single Rotation)**
2. **Left Rotation (Single Rotation)**
  ```

3. **Left-Right Rotation (Double Rotation)**
4. **Right-Left Rotation (Double Rotation)**

1. Right Rotation (Single Rotation)

Right rotation is used when a node becomes unbalanced due to a left child having a higher left subtree.

Before Rotation (Unbalanced):

markdown

```
    10
    /
   5
  /
 2
```

After Right Rotation:

markdown

```
   5
  / \
 2   10
```

2. Left Rotation (Single Rotation)

Left rotation is used when a node becomes unbalanced due to a right child having a higher right subtree.

Before Rotation (Unbalanced):

```
    2
     \
      5
       \
        10
```

After Left Rotation:

markdown

```
    5
   / \
  2   10
```

3. Left-Right Rotation (Double Rotation)

A left-right rotation is used when the left child has a right child that is heavier than the left child itself.

Before Rotation (Unbalanced):

markdown

```
      10
     /
    2
     \
```

```
    5
```

After Left-Right Rotation:

markdown

```
    5
   / \
  2   10
```

4. Right-Left Rotation (Double Rotation)

A right-left rotation is used when the right child has a left child that is heavier than the right child itself.

Before Rotation (Unbalanced):

markdown

```
  2
   \
    10
   /
  5
```

After Right-Left Rotation:

markdown

```
    5
   / \
```

2   10

Red-Black Trees

A **Red-Black Tree** is a binary search tree that satisfies the following properties to maintain balance:

1. Each node is either **red** or **black**.
2. The root node is always **black**.
3. Every leaf node (NIL node) is **black**.
4. If a red node has children, the children must be **black** (no two red nodes can be adjacent).
5. Every path from a node to its descendant NIL nodes must have the same number of black nodes (called the **black height**).
6. The root-to-leaf path must contain the same number of black nodes.

These properties help to maintain balance during insertion and deletion operations.

Rotations in Red-Black Trees

Red-Black Trees also use rotations to maintain balance, similar to AVL trees. However, Red-Black Trees have less strict balancing conditions, allowing for simpler and fewer rotations. The two basic rotations used are:

1. **Left Rotation**

2. **Right Rotation**

These rotations are used during insertions and deletions to maintain the Red-Black properties.

Practical Applications of AVL and Red-Black Trees

Balanced trees such as AVL and Red-Black Trees are widely used in scenarios where efficient searching, insertion, and deletion operations are required. Some practical applications include:

1. Databases

Balanced trees are often used to implement indexing structures for databases. Indexes allow for fast lookups, insertions, and deletions of records in large datasets. Both AVL and Red-Black Trees are commonly used in this context due to their ability to maintain logarithmic search times.

2. File Systems

File systems use balanced trees for indexing files and directories. For example, some modern file systems (e.g., B-trees, which are a type of balanced tree) use tree-based structures to organize files and allow for fast searches.

3. Memory Management

Balanced trees can be used to manage free blocks of memory in systems that support dynamic memory allocation. The tree ensures that memory is allocated and freed efficiently, without the need to search through all available memory.

4. Priority Queues

Balanced trees (especially Red-Black Trees) are used in the implementation of priority queues, where elements with the highest priority are dequeued first. Red-Black Trees provide efficient insertion, deletion, and lookup operations for managing priorities.

5. Network Routing

In networking, balanced trees can be used for efficient route lookup and management in routing tables. Balanced trees help store and retrieve routing information in logarithmic time, which is critical for high-performance networking.

6. Compiler Optimization

In compilers, balanced trees are used to implement **syntax trees** and **abstract syntax trees (AST)**, which represent the hierarchical structure of source code. These trees are crucial for optimizations during compilation, such as loop unrolling, constant folding, and expression evaluation.

Summary of Key Concepts:

- **Balanced Trees**: Balanced trees are binary search trees that maintain a balance condition to ensure efficient operations. They are crucial for ensuring logarithmic time complexity for insertions, deletions, and searches.
- **AVL Trees**: AVL trees maintain a strict balance condition (balance factor between -1 and 1) and use rotations to maintain balance.
- **Red-Black Trees**: Red-Black trees use color properties to maintain balance and ensure that no path from the root to a leaf is disproportionately long.
- **Rotations**: Rotations are used in both AVL and Red-Black trees to restore balance after insertion or deletion.
- **Practical Applications**: Balanced trees are used in databases, file systems, memory management, priority queues, network routing, and compiler optimizations.

Balanced trees, especially AVL and Red-Black trees, are fundamental in ensuring high performance for data structures that require frequent insertions, deletions, and lookups. Let me know if you'd like further clarification or more examples on any of these topics!

CHAPTER 13

TRIES (PREFIX TREES)

In this chapter, we will explore **tries** (also known as **prefix trees**), a specialized tree-based data structure used for efficient searching, insertion, and prefix matching. Tries are commonly used in applications like dictionary lookups and autocomplete systems, where efficiency in searching and prefix matching is critical.

Introduction to Tries

A **trie** is a tree-like data structure used to store a set of strings where each node represents a **single character** of a string. The key property of a trie is that it stores common prefixes of the strings once, saving space and allowing for efficient search operations.

In a trie, each path from the root to a leaf node corresponds to a **string**, and the edges represent the characters of the string. The **root** is an empty node, and every string is inserted by adding nodes corresponding to each character of the string.

Visual Representation of a Trie:

markdown

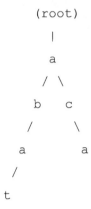

```
(root)
   |
   a
  / \
 b   c
 /    \
a      a
/
t
```

In this example, the trie stores the words "bat," "cat," and "cab." The common prefixes ("c" and "a") are stored only once, reducing duplication.

Efficient Searching with Tries

Tries allow for **efficient search operations** based on common prefixes. In a trie, searching for a word involves traversing the tree from the root, following the path corresponding to the characters of the word. If the path exists, the word is found; if not, the word is not in the trie.

Searching for a Word

To search for a word, you start from the root and follow the edges that correspond to each character in the word. If the entire word exists in the trie, you'll reach the end of the word at a node marked as a **leaf node** or an end-of-word marker.

Example: Searching for "cat"

- Start at the root.
- Follow the edge labeled "c" to the next node.
- Follow the edge labeled "a" to the next node.
- Follow the edge labeled "t" to the final node.

If all the edges exist, the word "cat" is in the trie.

Searching for a Prefix

One of the key features of tries is their ability to efficiently find words with a common prefix. Searching for a prefix works the same as searching for a word, but instead of checking if the word ends at a leaf node, you simply check if the entire prefix path exists.

For example, searching for the prefix "ca" will follow the path "c" → "a", and if this path exists, it means there are words that start with "ca" in the trie.

Insertion in a Trie

To insert a word into a trie, you start at the root and follow the path corresponding to the word's characters. If a character is missing in the current path, you create a new node for that character. After inserting all the characters, you mark the final

141

node as an **end-of-word marker** to signify that the word is complete.

Example: Inserting the word "bat" into a trie:

- Start at the root.
- "b" does not exist in the root's children, so create a node for "b".
- "a" does not exist as a child of "b", so create a node for "a".
- "t" does not exist as a child of "a", so create a node for "t".
- Mark the node for "t" as an end-of-word marker.

Visual Representation after Insertion:

markdown

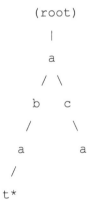

```
        (root)
          |
          a
        / \
       b   c
      /     \
     a       a
    /
   t*
```

The * next to "t" indicates the end of the word "bat."

Applications in Dictionary and Autocomplete Systems

Tries are particularly useful in applications that require **efficient string searching**, such as **dictionaries, autocomplete systems**, and **spell checkers**. They offer fast **prefix matching**, which is essential in these use cases.

1. Dictionary Systems

A trie can efficiently store a large set of words and allow for fast searching of whether a given word exists in the dictionary. Additionally, it supports searching for words that start with a given prefix, which is useful for autocompletion.

For instance, when you type the first few letters of a word in a dictionary app, the trie can quickly find all words starting with that prefix.

Example: Searching for "cat" in a dictionary trie would return:

- "cat"
- "cats"
- "catalog"
- "category"

2. Autocomplete Systems

Autocomplete systems use tries to provide suggestions as you type. When the user types a prefix, the trie can quickly find all the words that begin with that prefix. This is much faster than scanning an entire dictionary or database.

Example: For the prefix "ca", an autocomplete system could suggest:

- "cat"
- "cats"
- "cab"
- "candy"
- "california"

In this case, the system would follow the "ca" path in the trie and return all the words that extend from that prefix.

3. Spell Checking

Tries can also be used in spell checkers. When a user types a word, the trie can quickly check if the word exists in the dictionary. If the word is not found, the system can suggest the closest matching words based on their prefixes.

For example, if a user types "cat," the system checks if the word is in the trie. If not, it can suggest alternatives such as "bat," "hat," or "rat" based on common prefixes.

Advantages of Tries

1. **Efficient Prefix Searching**: Tries are very efficient at finding words that share a common prefix. This is especially useful in autocomplete systems, dictionary lookups, and other text-processing applications.

2. **Fast Search, Insert, and Delete Operations**: All of these operations can be performed in **O(k)** time, where **k** is the length of the word (not the number of words in the trie). This is more efficient than using a list or array for storing words.

3. **Space Efficiency**: By storing common prefixes only once, tries can save space compared to storing every word fully.

Disadvantages of Tries

1. **Memory Usage**: Although tries can be space-efficient when there are many common prefixes, they can still use significant memory, especially if the set of strings is sparse or the alphabet is large (e.g., storing words from all languages).

145

2. **Complexity**: Implementing and managing tries can be more complex than simpler data structures like arrays or hash maps.

Summary of Key Concepts:

- **Tries (Prefix Trees)**: A trie is a tree-like data structure that stores strings in a way that allows efficient searching, insertion, and prefix matching.
- **Efficient Searching**: Tries allow for quick search and prefix matching in **O(k)** time, where **k** is the length of the string being searched or inserted.
- **Applications**: Tries are widely used in applications such as **dictionary systems**, **autocomplete**, and **spell checking**, where fast prefix searching is required.
- **Rotations and Balancing**: Tries don't need balancing because each string is stored with respect to its prefix structure, making them particularly useful for text-based search tasks.

Tries are essential for applications that require fast prefix matching and efficient retrieval of strings, especially in scenarios involving large datasets like dictionaries or autocomplete systems. Let me know if you'd like further examples or explanations on any of these topics!

CHAPTER 14

GRAPHS: REPRESENTATION AND TRAVERSAL

In this chapter, we will explore **graphs,** one of the most versatile and widely used data structures in computer science. We will cover how graphs are represented, how to traverse them efficiently using **Depth-First Search (DFS)** and **Breadth-First Search (BFS),** and discuss practical applications of graph traversal in various fields.

Graph Representation: Adjacency Matrix and Adjacency List

A **graph** is a collection of **vertices (nodes)** connected by **edges (arcs).** Graphs can be classified into different types based on edge direction (directed or undirected) and edge weights (weighted or unweighted). For example, a graph could represent a network of cities connected by roads (vertices are cities, edges are roads).

Graphs can be represented in multiple ways, but the two most common methods are the **adjacency matrix** and **adjacency list**.

1. Adjacency Matrix

An **adjacency matrix** is a 2D array that represents a graph. If there are **n** vertices, the adjacency matrix is an **n x n** matrix. Each element `matrix[i][j]` represents the presence or absence of an edge between vertex `i` and vertex `j`.

- For an undirected graph, if there is an edge between `i` and `j`, then `matrix[i][j]` and `matrix[j][i]` are set to `1` (or the edge weight in a weighted graph). If there is no edge, the value is `0`.
- For a directed graph, `matrix[i][j]` indicates whether there is a directed edge from vertex `i` to vertex `j`.

Example (Undirected Graph):

less

```
A - B
|   |
C - D
```

The adjacency matrix for this graph (with vertices A, B, C, D) looks like:

css

```
    A  B  C  D
A  [ 0, 1, 1, 0 ]
```

148

```
B   [ 1,  0,  0,  1 ]
C   [ 1,  0,  0,  1 ]
D   [ 0,  1,  1,  0 ]
```

Example (Directed Graph):

css

```
    A → B
    ↓   ↑
    C ← D
```

The adjacency matrix for this directed graph looks like:

css

```
      A   B   C   D
A   [ 0,  1,  1,  0 ]
B   [ 0,  0,  0,  1 ]
C   [ 0,  0,  0,  0 ]
D   [ 0,  0,  1,  0 ]
```

2. Adjacency List

An **adjacency list** is a more space-efficient representation, especially for sparse graphs. It consists of an array of lists (or vectors) where each index represents a vertex, and the list at that index contains all the vertices that are adjacent to the vertex.

For an undirected graph, the adjacency list for the graph:

149

less

```
A - B
|   |
C - D
```

would look like this:

css

```
A → [B, C]
B → [A, D]
C → [A, D]
D → [B, C]
```

For a directed graph:

css

```
A → B
↓   ↑
C ← D
```

the adjacency list would be:

css

```
A → [B, C]
B → [D]
C → []
```

```
D → [C]
```

The adjacency list is often more space-efficient than the adjacency matrix for sparse graphs because it only stores the edges that exist.

Depth-First Search (DFS) and Breadth-First Search (BFS)

Graph traversal algorithms are used to visit all the vertices and edges in a graph. Two common traversal techniques are **Depth-First Search (DFS)** and **Breadth-First Search (BFS)**.

1. Depth-First Search (DFS)

DFS explores as far down a branch of the graph as possible before backtracking. It uses a **stack** (either explicitly or via recursion) to remember the vertices to visit.

Steps of DFS:

1. Start from a given vertex and mark it as visited.
2. Recursively visit all the adjacent vertices that haven't been visited.
3. Backtrack when no unvisited adjacent vertices are found.

DFS can be implemented using recursion or an explicit stack.

DFS Algorithm:

1. Start at the root (or any arbitrary node) and mark it as visited.
2. Visit all its adjacent nodes that haven't been visited, using a stack to keep track of the nodes to visit next.

DFS Example (C++ Code):

cpp

```cpp
#include <iostream>
#include <vector>
#include <stack>
using namespace std;

class Graph {
public:
    int V;
    vector<int>* adj;

    Graph(int v) {
        V = v;
        adj = new vector<int>[v];
    }

    void addEdge(int u, int v) {
        adj[u].push_back(v);
    }

    void DFS(int start) {
```

```cpp
        vector<bool> visited(V, false);
        stack<int> s;
        s.push(start);
        visited[start] = true;

        while (!s.empty()) {
            int node = s.top();
            s.pop();
            cout << node << " ";

            // Visit all unvisited adjacent
vertices
            for (int i = 0; i < adj[node].size();
i++) {
                int v = adj[node][i];
                if (!visited[v]) {
                    visited[v] = true;
                    s.push(v);
                }
            }
        }
        cout << endl;
    }
};

int main() {
    Graph g(5);
    g.addEdge(0, 1);
    g.addEdge(0, 2);
```

```
g.addEdge(1, 3);
g.addEdge(1, 4);

cout << "DFS starting from vertex 0: ";
g.DFS(0);   // Output: 0 2 1 4 3

return 0;
}
```

Explanation:

- The DFS function uses a stack to explore the graph. It starts from the start node, marks it as visited, and then visits all adjacent nodes recursively.

2. Breadth-First Search (BFS)

BFS explores the graph level by level, starting from the root (or any arbitrary node), visiting all the adjacent nodes first before moving on to the next level.

BFS uses a **queue** to remember the nodes to visit.

Steps of BFS:

1. Start from the root (or any arbitrary node) and mark it as visited.
2. Visit all adjacent nodes, adding them to a queue.

3. Dequeue nodes from the front of the queue, visiting their unvisited neighbors and adding them to the queue.

BFS Algorithm:

1. Start at the root node, mark it as visited, and enqueue it.
2. While the queue is not empty, dequeue a node, and visit all of its adjacent unvisited nodes, enqueuing them.

BFS Example (C++ Code):

cpp

```cpp
#include <iostream>
#include <vector>
#include <queue>
using namespace std;

class Graph {
public:
    int V;
    vector<int>* adj;

    Graph(int v) {
        V = v;
        adj = new vector<int>[v];
    }

    void addEdge(int u, int v) {
```

```cpp
        adj[u].push_back(v);
    }

    void BFS(int start) {
        vector<bool> visited(V, false);
        queue<int> q;
        q.push(start);
        visited[start] = true;

        while (!q.empty()) {
            int node = q.front();
            q.pop();
            cout << node << " ";

            // Visit all unvisited adjacent
vertices
            for (int i = 0; i < adj[node].size();
i++) {
                int v = adj[node][i];
                if (!visited[v]) {
                    visited[v] = true;
                    q.push(v);
                }
            }
        }
        cout << endl;
    }
};
```

```
int main() {
    Graph g(5);
    g.addEdge(0, 1);
    g.addEdge(0, 2);
    g.addEdge(1, 3);
    g.addEdge(1, 4);

    cout << "BFS starting from vertex 0: ";
    g.BFS(0);   // Output: 0 1 2 3 4

    return 0;
}
```

Explanation:

- The BFS function uses a queue to explore the graph. It starts from the start node, marks it as visited, and then visits all adjacent nodes level by level.

Applications of Graph Traversal

Graph traversal techniques like DFS and BFS have a wide range of applications in various domains:

1. Pathfinding Algorithms

Graph traversal is the foundation for pathfinding algorithms like **Dijkstra's algorithm** and *A search algorithm**, which are used to

157

find the shortest path between nodes in a graph (e.g., in maps and network routing).

2. Web Crawlers

Web crawlers use graph traversal to explore websites. Websites are represented as graphs, where pages are nodes and hyperlinks are edges. BFS is commonly used in crawlers to visit all pages starting from a root page.

3. Social Network Analysis

In social networks, nodes represent users, and edges represent relationships. Graph traversal algorithms can be used to find relationships between users, detect communities, and analyze networks.

4. Dependency Resolution

In package management systems, graphs are used to represent dependencies between packages. BFS or DFS can be used to determine the order in which packages should be installed or uninstalled.

5. Puzzle Solving

Graph traversal is used in solving puzzles like **maze solving**. The maze is represented as a graph, and BFS or DFS can be used to find a path from the start to the goal.

6. Network Flow Algorithms

Graph traversal is also used in network flow algorithms like **Ford-Fulkerson** for computing maximum flow in a network.

Summary of Key Concepts:

- **Graph Representation**: Graphs can be represented using an **adjacency matrix** or an **adjacency list**. The adjacency matrix is more space-intensive but useful for dense graphs, while the adjacency list is more space-efficient for sparse graphs.
- **DFS**: **Depth-First Search (DFS)** explores as far as possible along a branch before backtracking. It uses a stack and can be implemented recursively.
- **BFS**: **Breadth-First Search (BFS)** explores nodes level by level, using a queue. It is often used for finding the shortest path in an unweighted graph.
- **Applications**: Graph traversal is used in various applications such as **pathfinding**, **web crawling**, **social network analysis**, and **network flow algorithms**.

Graph traversal is a powerful tool for working with complex data structures that represent relationships between entities. Let me know if you'd like further details or examples on any of these topics!

CHAPTER 15

SORTING ALGORITHMS: FROM SIMPLE TO ADVANCED

In this chapter, we will explore **sorting algorithms**, which are fundamental techniques used to arrange data in a particular order, typically in **ascending** or **descending** order. Sorting is one of the most common operations in computer science and is essential for many algorithms, including search algorithms, data analysis, and database management systems. We will cover a variety of sorting algorithms, from simple ones like **bubble sort**, **selection sort**, and **insertion sort**, to more advanced ones like **merge sort**, **quick sort**, and **heap sort**.

Introduction to Sorting Algorithms

A **sorting algorithm** takes a list (or array) of elements and arranges them in a specific order (typically in **ascending** or **descending** order). Sorting is important because it enables faster searching, improves data organization, and helps with efficient use of other algorithms that require ordered data.

There are several sorting algorithms, each with different **time complexity**, **space complexity**, and **performance characteristics**. We'll examine these algorithms based on their efficiency, starting with simpler ones and progressing to more advanced algorithms.

Bubble Sort, Selection Sort, Insertion Sort

These three algorithms are considered basic and easy to implement but are inefficient for large datasets due to their **O(n²)** time complexity.

1. Bubble Sort

Bubble Sort is the simplest sorting algorithm, where each element in the list is compared with the adjacent one, and the two are swapped if they are in the wrong order. This process is repeated until no more swaps are needed.

Algorithm Steps:

1. Traverse the list from the beginning.
2. Compare adjacent elements, swapping them if they are in the wrong order.
3. Continue the process for each element until the entire list is sorted.

C++ Code for Bubble Sort:

cpp

```cpp
#include <iostream>
using namespace std;

void bubbleSort(int arr[], int n) {
    for (int i = 0; i < n-1; i++) {
        for (int j = 0; j < n-i-1; j++) {
            if (arr[j] > arr[j+1]) {
                swap(arr[j], arr[j+1]);  // Swap
if the element is in the wrong order
            }
        }
    }
}

int main() {
    int arr[] = {64, 34, 25, 12, 22, 11, 90};
    int n = sizeof(arr)/sizeof(arr[0]);

    bubbleSort(arr, n);

    cout << "Sorted array: ";
    for (int i = 0; i < n; i++) {
        cout << arr[i] << " ";
    }
    cout << endl;

    return 0;
}
```

Time Complexity: $O(n^2)$, where n is the number of elements. The worst-case and average case both have quadratic time complexity.

2. Selection Sort

Selection Sort works by repeatedly finding the smallest (or largest, depending on order) element from the unsorted portion of the list and swapping it with the first unsorted element. This process is repeated for the remaining unsorted part.

Algorithm Steps:

1. Start from the first element and search for the smallest element in the unsorted part of the list.
2. Swap the smallest element found with the first unsorted element.
3. Repeat the process for the rest of the list.

C++ Code for Selection Sort:

cpp

```
#include <iostream>
using namespace std;

void selectionSort(int arr[], int n) {
    for (int i = 0; i < n-1; i++) {
        int minIndex = i;
        for (int j = i+1; j < n; j++) {
```

```cpp
            if (arr[j] < arr[minIndex]) {
                minIndex = j;
            }
        }
        swap(arr[i], arr[minIndex]);
    }
}

int main() {
    int arr[] = {64, 25, 12, 22, 11};
    int n = sizeof(arr)/sizeof(arr[0]);

    selectionSort(arr, n);

    cout << "Sorted array: ";
    for (int i = 0; i < n; i++) {
        cout << arr[i] << " ";
    }
    cout << endl;

    return 0;
}
```

Time Complexity: $O(n^2)$, because it involves two nested loops: one to find the minimum element and the other to compare the remaining elements.

3. Insertion Sort

Insertion Sort works by building a sorted part of the list one element at a time. It takes each element from the unsorted portion of the list and inserts it into the correct position in the sorted portion.

Algorithm Steps:

1. Start with the second element (since the first element is trivially sorted).
2. Compare the current element with the elements in the sorted part of the list and shift them as necessary.
3. Insert the current element in the correct position.

C++ Code for Insertion Sort:

cpp

```cpp
#include <iostream>
using namespace std;

void insertionSort(int arr[], int n) {
    for (int i = 1; i < n; i++) {
        int key = arr[i];
        int j = i - 1;

        // Shift elements of the sorted portion
that are greater than key
```

```cpp
        while (j >= 0 && arr[j] > key) {
            arr[j + 1] = arr[j];
            j--;
        }

        arr[j + 1] = key;
    }
}

int main() {
    int arr[] = {12, 11, 13, 5, 6};
    int n = sizeof(arr)/sizeof(arr[0]);

    insertionSort(arr, n);

    cout << "Sorted array: ";
    for (int i = 0; i < n; i++) {
        cout << arr[i] << " ";
    }
    cout << endl;

    return 0;
}
```

Time Complexity: $O(n^2)$ in the worst case, but $O(n)$ in the best case when the list is already sorted. The average-case time complexity is $O(n^2)$.

Merge Sort, Quick Sort, Heap Sort

167

These are more advanced sorting algorithms that have better performance characteristics than bubble sort, selection sort, and insertion sort. They have an average and worst-case time complexity of O(n log n), making them more efficient for larger datasets.

4. Merge Sort

Merge Sort is a **divide-and-conquer** algorithm. It works by recursively dividing the list into two halves, sorting each half, and then merging the two sorted halves back together.

Algorithm Steps:

1. Split the array into two halves.
2. Recursively sort each half.
3. Merge the two sorted halves.

C++ Code for Merge Sort:

cpp

```cpp
#include <iostream>
using namespace std;

void merge(int arr[], int left, int right) {
    if (left >= right) return;

    int mid = left + (right - left) / 2;
```

```
    merge(arr, left, mid);  // Left half
    merge(arr, mid + 1, right);  // Right half

    int n1 = mid - left + 1;
    int n2 = right - mid;

    int L[n1], R[n2];
    for (int i = 0; i < n1; i++) L[i] = arr[left
+ i];
    for (int i = 0; i < n2; i++) R[i] = arr[mid
+ 1 + i];

    int i = 0, j = 0, k = left;
    while (i < n1 && j < n2) {
        if (L[i] <= R[j]) {
            arr[k] = L[i];
            i++;
        } else {
            arr[k] = R[j];
            j++;
        }
        k++;
    }

    while (i < n1) {
        arr[k] = L[i];
        i++;
        k++;
    }
```

```cpp
        while (j < n2) {
            arr[k] = R[j];
            j++;
            k++;
        }
    }

int main() {
    int arr[] = {12, 11, 13, 5, 6, 7};
    int n = sizeof(arr)/sizeof(arr[0]);

    merge(arr, 0, n-1);

    cout << "Sorted array: ";
    for (int i = 0; i < n; i++) {
        cout << arr[i] << " ";
    }
    cout << endl;

    return 0;
}
```

Time Complexity: O(n log n) for both average and worst-case scenarios. Merge Sort is stable and guarantees O(n log n) performance.

5. Quick Sort

Quick Sort is another **divide-and-conquer** algorithm. It works by selecting a **pivot** element, partitioning the array into two halves (one with elements smaller than the pivot and one with elements greater), and then recursively sorting each half.

Algorithm Steps:

1. Select a pivot element.
2. Partition the array around the pivot, placing smaller elements on the left and larger elements on the right.
3. Recursively apply the same process to the left and right subarrays.

C++ Code for Quick Sort:

cpp

```cpp
#include <iostream>
using namespace std;

int partition(int arr[], int low, int high) {
    int pivot = arr[high];
    int i = low - 1;

    for (int j = low; j < high; j++) {
        if (arr[j] < pivot) {
            i++;
```

171

```cpp
            swap(arr[i], arr[j]);
        }
    }

    swap(arr[i + 1], arr[high]);
    return i + 1;
}

void quickSort(int arr[], int low, int high) {
    if (low < high) {
        int pi = partition(arr, low, high);
        quickSort(arr, low, pi - 1);
        quickSort(arr, pi + 1, high);
    }
}

int main() {
    int arr[] = {10, 7, 8, 9, 1, 5};
    int n = sizeof(arr)/sizeof(arr[0]);

    quickSort(arr, 0, n - 1);

    cout << "Sorted array: ";
    for (int i = 0; i < n; i++) {
        cout << arr[i] << " ";
    }
    cout << endl;

    return 0;
```

```
}
```

Time Complexity: O(n log n) on average, but O(n²) in the worst case when the pivot is poorly chosen (e.g., always the smallest or largest element).

6. Heap Sort

Heap Sort is based on a **binary heap** data structure (either a max-heap or a min-heap). It works by first building a heap from the input data and then repeatedly extracting the maximum element (or minimum for a min-heap) to build the sorted list.

Algorithm Steps:

1. Build a max-heap from the input array.
2. Repeatedly extract the maximum element from the heap and move it to the end of the array.
3. Restore the heap property after each extraction.

C++ Code for Heap Sort:

cpp

```cpp
#include <iostream>
using namespace std;

void heapify(int arr[], int n, int i) {
    int largest = i;
```

```cpp
    int left = 2 * i + 1;
    int right = 2 * i + 2;

    if (left < n && arr[left] > arr[largest])
largest = left;
    if (right < n && arr[right] > arr[largest])
largest = right;

    if (largest != i) {
        swap(arr[i], arr[largest]);
        heapify(arr, n, largest);
    }
}

void heapSort(int arr[], int n) {
    for (int i = n / 2 - 1; i >= 0; i--)
heapify(arr, n, i);
    for (int i = n - 1; i >= 1; i--) {
        swap(arr[0], arr[i]);
        heapify(arr, i, 0);
    }
}

int main() {
    int arr[] = {12, 11, 13, 5, 6, 7};
    int n = sizeof(arr)/sizeof(arr[0]);

    heapSort(arr, n);
```

```cpp
cout << "Sorted array: ";
for (int i = 0; i < n; i++) {
    cout << arr[i] << " ";
}
cout << endl;

return 0;
}
```

Time Complexity: O(n log n) for both the average and worst-case scenarios. Heap Sort is not a stable sort.

Summary of Key Concepts:

- **Bubble Sort, Selection Sort, and Insertion Sort**: These simple sorting algorithms are easy to implement but have O(n²) time complexity, making them inefficient for large datasets.

- **Merge Sort, Quick Sort, and Heap Sort**: These advanced algorithms are more efficient with an average and worst-case time complexity of O(n log n). Merge Sort is stable, Quick Sort is faster on average, and Heap Sort works well for large datasets.

Sorting algorithms are essential in computer science, and choosing the right algorithm depends on the dataset size, stability requirements, and worst-case performance. Let me know if you'd like more examples or clarifications!

CHAPTER 16

SEARCHING ALGORITHMS

In this chapter, we will explore **searching algorithms**, which are fundamental for locating a specific element in a collection of data. Searching is a critical operation in many applications, such as databases, search engines, and file systems. We will discuss basic **searching techniques** like **linear search** and **binary search**, as well as **advanced searching techniques** and the differences in searching **sorted** versus **unsorted** data.

Linear Search vs Binary Search

Two of the most commonly used search algorithms are **linear search** and **binary search**. These algorithms differ significantly in their efficiency, depending on whether the data is sorted or unsorted.

1. Linear Search

Linear search is the simplest searching algorithm. It works by sequentially checking each element in a list or array until the desired element is found or the entire list has been searched.

Algorithm Steps:

1. Start from the first element of the list.

2. Compare the current element with the target value.

3. If the element matches the target, return the index.

4. If the element does not match, move to the next element.

5. Repeat steps 2-4 until the target is found or the list is exhausted.

C++ Code for Linear Search:

cpp

```cpp
#include <iostream>
using namespace std;

int linearSearch(int arr[], int n, int target) {
    for (int i = 0; i < n; i++) {
        if (arr[i] == target) {
            return i;   // Element found at index i
        }
    }
    return -1;   // Element not found
}

int main() {
    int arr[] = {5, 3, 7, 1, 9};
    int n = sizeof(arr)/sizeof(arr[0]);
    int target = 7;
```

```
int result = linearSearch(arr, n, target);
if (result != -1)
    cout << "Element found at index " <<
result << endl;
else
    cout << "Element not found" << endl;

return 0;
}
```

Time Complexity: O(n), where n is the number of elements in the array. Linear search is inefficient for large datasets, as it may require checking every element.

2. Binary Search

Binary search is a more efficient searching algorithm that works on **sorted arrays** or lists. It repeatedly divides the search space in half, which allows it to find the target in logarithmic time.

Algorithm Steps:

1. Start by examining the middle element of the array.
2. If the middle element matches the target, return its index.
3. If the target is less than the middle element, repeat the search on the left half.
4. If the target is greater than the middle element, repeat the search on the right half.

5. Repeat this process until the target is found or the search space is empty.

C++ Code for Binary Search:

cpp

```cpp
#include <iostream>
using namespace std;

int binarySearch(int arr[], int n, int target) {
    int left = 0;
    int right = n - 1;

    while (left <= right) {
        int mid = left + (right - left) / 2;

        // Check if target is at the middle
        if (arr[mid] == target) {
            return mid;
        }

        // If target is smaller, search the left
half
        if (arr[mid] > target) {
            right = mid - 1;
        }
        // If target is larger, search the right
half
```

```cpp
        else {
            left = mid + 1;
        }
    }
    return -1;  // Target not found
}


int main() {
    int arr[] = {1, 3, 5, 7, 9};
    int n = sizeof(arr)/sizeof(arr[0]);
    int target = 7;

    int result = binarySearch(arr, n, target);
    if (result != -1)
        cout << "Element found at index " <<
result << endl;
    else
        cout << "Element not found" << endl;

    return 0;
}
```

Time Complexity: O(log n), where n is the number of elements in the array. Binary search is much faster than linear search for large datasets, but it only works on sorted data.

Advanced Searching Techniques

While linear search and binary search are the most common searching algorithms, there are several advanced searching techniques designed to improve search performance under certain conditions.

1. Hashing

Hashing is an advanced technique where a **hash function** is used to map a search key to an index in a hash table. Hashing provides **O(1)** average time complexity for searching, as it directly computes the index of the target element. However, it requires more memory and may suffer from **collisions** (when two keys map to the same index).

Example: A **hash map** is used in many applications to provide constant-time lookups.

2. Jump Search

Jump Search is an algorithm that works by dividing the data into smaller blocks of fixed size and performing a linear search within these blocks. It then jumps ahead by a fixed number of steps to find the potential block where the target might be located.

Time Complexity: $O(\sqrt{n})$. Jump search is a compromise between linear and binary search and is suitable for sorted arrays or lists.

3. Interpolation Search

Interpolation Search is an improvement over binary search for uniformly distributed data. Instead of dividing the search space into equal halves, interpolation search estimates where the target might be based on its value and the values of the first and last elements of the array.

Time Complexity: $O(\log \log n)$ in the best case, but $O(n)$ in the worst case.

4. Exponential Search

Exponential Search (also known as **exponential binary search**) is used when the range of elements is unknown. It first finds the range where the target may exist by exponentially increasing the index and then applies binary search within the identified range.

Time Complexity: $O(\log n)$.

Searching in Sorted vs Unsorted Data

The performance of searching algorithms depends on whether the data is **sorted** or **unsorted**.

1. Searching in Unsorted Data

When the data is unsorted, the most straightforward approach is **linear search**. Since there is no ordering, the algorithm must examine each element one by one to determine if it matches the target. Other advanced techniques like **hashing** can be used to improve performance for repeated search operations, but they still require additional space.

- **Linear Search**: O(n)
- **Hashing**: O(1) (average case), but requires extra space.

2. Searching in Sorted Data

If the data is **sorted**, more efficient algorithms like **binary search** can be used. Sorting the data first and then applying binary search is a good strategy for large datasets. Other advanced techniques like **jump search** or **interpolation search** can also be used, depending on the properties of the data.

- **Binary Search**: O(log n)
- **Jump Search**: O($\sqrt{n}$)
- **Interpolation Search**: O(log log n) (for uniformly distributed data)

If the data is frequently updated and needs to be kept sorted, advanced data structures such as **balanced binary search trees** (e.g., AVL trees, Red-Black trees) or **B-trees** may be used to maintain sorted order while providing efficient search operations.

Summary of Key Concepts:

- **Linear Search**: A simple algorithm with a time complexity of $O(n)$, suitable for unsorted data but inefficient for large datasets.

- **Binary Search**: A more efficient algorithm with a time complexity of $O(\log n)$, but it only works on sorted data.

- **Advanced Searching Techniques**: Include **hashing** ($O(1)$ average case), **jump search** ($O(\sqrt{n})$), **interpolation search** ($O(\log \log n)$), and **exponential search** ($O(\log n)$).

- **Searching in Sorted Data**: Efficient algorithms like **binary search** are used for searching in sorted data, providing better performance than linear search.

- **Searching in Unsorted Data**: **Linear search** is often used for unsorted data, though **hashing** can be employed for faster lookups in some cases.

Choosing the right searching algorithm depends on whether the data is sorted or unsorted, the size of the dataset, and the need for efficiency in repeated search operations. Let me know if you need more details or examples for any of these topics!

CHAPTER 17

DYNAMIC PROGRAMMING: SOLVING COMPLEX PROBLEMS

In this chapter, we will explore **dynamic programming (DP)**, a powerful technique for solving complex problems by breaking them down into simpler subproblems. Dynamic programming is particularly useful for optimization problems where a solution can be recursively defined. We will also compare two main techniques of dynamic programming: **memoization** and **tabulation**. Lastly, we will explore real-world problems that can be solved using dynamic programming, such as the **Fibonacci sequence** and the **knapsack problem**.

Introduction to Dynamic Programming

Dynamic programming (DP) is an algorithmic technique used for solving problems that can be divided into overlapping subproblems. It is used when a problem has:

- **Optimal substructure**: The optimal solution to the problem can be constructed from optimal solutions to its subproblems.
- **Overlapping subproblems**: The problem can be broken down into subproblems that are solved repeatedly.

185

Dynamic programming stores the results of subproblems to avoid redundant calculations, leading to a significant reduction in time complexity. The key idea is to **store solutions to subproblems** in a data structure (like an array or a table) so that they can be reused in future computations, avoiding redundant work.

There are two main approaches to dynamic programming:

1. **Memoization** (Top-down approach)
2. **Tabulation** (Bottom-up approach)

Memoization vs Tabulation

1. Memoization (Top-Down Approach)

Memoization is a top-down approach where we recursively solve the problem and store the results of subproblems in a data structure (like an array or hash map) so that we do not recompute them. Whenever a subproblem is encountered, we first check if it has already been solved and stored; if so, we simply return the stored result.

Key points about Memoization:

- It is a recursive approach that starts solving the problem from the top (starting with the main problem) and breaks it down into subproblems.
- The results of subproblems are stored in a cache (e.g., an array or a hash map) to avoid recalculating them.

Example: Fibonacci Sequence using Memoization:

cpp

```cpp
#include <iostream>
#include <unordered_map>
using namespace std;

unordered_map<int, long long> memo;

long long fibonacci(int n) {
    // Base case
    if (n <= 1) return n;

    // Check if result is already computed
    if (memo.find(n) != memo.end()) return
memo[n];

    // Recursive call
    memo[n] = fibonacci(n - 1) + fibonacci(n -
2);

    return memo[n];
}

int main() {
    int n = 50; // Example Fibonacci number
    cout << "Fibonacci(" << n << ") = " <<
fibonacci(n) << endl;
    return 0;
```

```
}
```

Time Complexity: O(n), as each subproblem is solved only once and stored in the cache.

2. Tabulation (Bottom-Up Approach)

Tabulation is the bottom-up approach where we solve the problem iteratively, starting from the base case and working our way up to the final solution. We store the results of subproblems in a table (typically an array) and iteratively fill it in a bottom-up manner.

Key points about Tabulation:

- It is an iterative approach that builds solutions to subproblems in a tabular form (usually an array or matrix).
- It is generally more space-efficient than memoization because it avoids recursion, but it requires more careful setup of the table.

Example: Fibonacci Sequence using Tabulation:

cpp

```cpp
#include <iostream>
using namespace std;
```

```cpp
long long fibonacci(int n) {
    if (n <= 1) return n;

    long long dp[n + 1];    // Table to store
Fibonacci numbers

    dp[0] = 0;
    dp[1] = 1;

    for (int i = 2; i <= n; i++) {
        dp[i] = dp[i - 1] + dp[i - 2];
    }

    return dp[n];
}

int main() {
    int n = 50;   // Example Fibonacci number
    cout << "Fibonacci(" << n << ") = " <<
fibonacci(n) << endl;
    return 0;
}
```

Time Complexity: O(n), as each subproblem is solved once in an iterative manner.

Space Complexity: O(n) due to the storage required for the table.

189

Real-World Problems Solved with Dynamic Programming

Dynamic programming is a versatile technique used to solve many real-world optimization problems. Here are a few classic examples of problems that can be solved using dynamic programming.

1. Fibonacci Sequence

The **Fibonacci sequence** is a series of numbers where each number is the sum of the two preceding ones, starting from 0 and 1. The sequence is defined as:

- $F(0) = 0$
- $F(1) = 1$
- $F(n) = F(n-1) + F(n-2)$

Using dynamic programming, we can compute the Fibonacci sequence efficiently by either memoization or tabulation.

2. The Knapsack Problem

The **0/1 knapsack problem** is a classic optimization problem where you are given a set of items, each with a weight and a value, and a knapsack with a maximum weight capacity. The goal is to determine the maximum value you can fit into the knapsack without exceeding the capacity.

Dynamic Programming Solution: We use a table to store the maximum value that can be achieved for each weight capacity from 0 to W (where W is the maximum weight capacity of the knapsack).

Algorithm Steps:

1. Define a 2D table where dp[i][w] represents the maximum value that can be achieved using the first i items with a weight limit of w.
2. Iterate through each item and each weight capacity, filling the table based on whether to include or exclude the current item.

Example: Knapsack Problem using Dynamic Programming:

cpp

```cpp
#include <iostream>
#include <vector>
using namespace std;

int knapsack(int W, vector<int>& weights,
vector<int>& values, int n) {
    vector<vector<int>> dp(n + 1, vector<int>(W
+ 1, 0));

    // Build the DP table
    for (int i = 1; i <= n; i++) {
```

191

```cpp
        for (int w = 1; w <= W; w++) {
            if (weights[i - 1] <= w) {
                dp[i][w] = max(dp[i - 1][w], dp[i
- 1][w - weights[i - 1]] + values[i - 1]);
            } else {
                dp[i][w] = dp[i - 1][w];
            }
        }
    }

    return dp[n][W];
}


int main() {
    int W = 50;   // Maximum weight of knapsack
    vector<int> values = {60, 100, 120};   //
Values of items
    vector<int> weights = {10, 20, 30};   //
Weights of items
    int n = values.size();


    cout << "Maximum value in Knapsack = " <<
knapsack(W, weights, values, n) << endl;


    return 0;
}
```

Time Complexity: O(n * W), where n is the number of items and W is the weight capacity of the knapsack.

Space Complexity: O(n * W) due to the 2D table used to store intermediate results.

3. Longest Common Subsequence (LCS)

The **Longest Common Subsequence (LCS)** problem is used to find the longest subsequence common to two sequences (e.g., strings). Unlike substrings, subsequences don't have to be contiguous but must preserve the order of characters.

Dynamic Programming Solution:

1. Define a 2D table `dp[i][j]` that represents the length of the longest common subsequence between the first `i` characters of one string and the first `j` characters of another.
2. Fill the table iteratively based on whether characters from both strings match.

Example: LCS using Dynamic Programming:

cpp

```cpp
#include <iostream>
#include <vector>
using namespace std;

int lcs(string X, string Y) {
    int m = X.size();
```

```cpp
    int n = Y.size();

    vector<vector<int>> dp(m + 1, vector<int>(n
+ 1, 0));

    // Build the DP table
    for (int i = 1; i <= m; i++) {
        for (int j = 1; j <= n; j++) {
            if (X[i - 1] == Y[j - 1]) {
                dp[i][j] = dp[i - 1][j - 1] + 1;
            } else {
                dp[i][j]  =  max(dp[i  -  1][j],
dp[i][j - 1]);
            }
        }
    }

    return dp[m][n];
}

int main() {
    string X = "AGGTAB";
    string Y = "GXTXAYB";

    cout << "Length of LCS: " << lcs(X, Y) <<
endl;  // Output: 4

    return 0;
}
```

194

Time Complexity: O(m * n), where m and n are the lengths of the two strings.

Summary of Key Concepts:

- **Dynamic Programming (DP)**: A technique for solving problems by breaking them down into overlapping subproblems and storing their solutions to avoid redundant work.
- **Memoization vs. Tabulation**: Memoization uses recursion and stores solutions to subproblems in a cache (top-down), while tabulation builds a table iteratively (bottom-up).
- **Applications**: DP is used in a wide variety of problems, such as the **Fibonacci sequence**, the **knapsack problem**, **LCS**, and many optimization problems.

Dynamic programming is a powerful tool for solving problems with overlapping subproblems and optimal substructure, and it plays a crucial role in real-world applications like scheduling, resource allocation, and optimization. Let me know if you'd like more examples or details!

CHAPTER 18

GREEDY ALGORITHMS

In this chapter, we will explore **greedy algorithms**, a class of algorithms that make **locally optimal** choices at each step with the hope of finding a globally optimal solution. While greedy algorithms do not always guarantee the best solution in all cases, they are very effective for solving certain types of problems, especially when the problem exhibits the **greedy-choice property** and **optimal substructure**.

Understanding the Greedy Approach

A **greedy algorithm** is an approach for solving problems by choosing the best option available at each step, without reconsidering previous choices. It makes the **locally optimal choice** in the hope that these local choices will lead to a globally optimal solution.

Greedy-Choice Property

The greedy-choice property means that a globally optimal solution can be arrived at by selecting a locally optimal choice at each step. This property holds for some problems but not for all.

Optimal Substructure

A problem has optimal substructure if an optimal solution to the problem can be constructed efficiently from optimal solutions to its subproblems. This is a common characteristic of problems that can be solved using greedy algorithms.

Greedy Algorithms: Key Steps

1. **Problem Decomposition**: Break the problem into smaller subproblems.
2. **Selection**: Make a locally optimal choice for each subproblem.
3. **Feasibility Check**: Ensure that the selected choice doesn't violate any constraints.
4. **Solution Construction**: Combine the solutions to the subproblems to form a final solution.

Real-World Examples of Greedy Algorithms

Now let's discuss a couple of common real-world problems that can be solved using greedy algorithms: **coin change problem** and **activity selection problem**.

1. Coin Change Problem

The **coin change problem** involves determining the minimum number of coins required to make a given amount of change.

Given an unlimited supply of coins with specific denominations, the goal is to find the fewest number of coins needed to make the target amount.

Greedy Approach:

- At each step, choose the **largest coin denomination** that is less than or equal to the remaining amount.
- Repeat this process until the remaining amount becomes zero.

Example: Given coin denominations {1, 5, 10, 25} and a target amount of 30, the greedy approach would choose:

1. Take one coin of denomination 25 (remaining amount = 5).
2. Take one coin of denomination 5 (remaining amount = 0).

Thus, the minimum number of coins needed is 2.

C++ Code for Coin Change Problem using Greedy Algorithm:

cpp

```cpp
#include <iostream>
#include <vector>
#include <algorithm>
using namespace std;
```

```cpp
int   coinChangeGreedy(vector<int>&   coins,   int
amount) {
    int coinCount = 0;

    // Sort the coins in descending order
    sort(coins.rbegin(), coins.rend());

    for (int coin : coins) {
        if (amount == 0) break;
        if (coin <= amount) {
            coinCount += amount / coin;   // Use
as many coins of this denomination as possible
            amount %= coin;      // Update the
remaining amount
        }
    }

    return coinCount;
}

int main() {
    vector<int> coins = {1, 5, 10, 25};   // Coin
denominations
    int amount = 30;   // Amount to be changed

    cout << "Minimum number of coins required: "
<< coinChangeGreedy(coins, amount) << endl;

    return 0;
```

}

Time Complexity: O(n log n) due to the sorting step, where n is the number of coin denominations. The greedy part (iterating through the coins) has a complexity of O(n).

Note: The greedy algorithm works perfectly for certain coin denominations (e.g., when denominations are powers of 2), but it might not give the optimal solution in other cases (e.g., when denominations are arbitrary).

2. Activity Selection Problem

The **activity selection problem** involves selecting the maximum number of non-overlapping activities from a set of activities. Each activity has a start time and finish time, and the goal is to select as many activities as possible without any two activities overlapping.

Greedy Approach:

- Sort the activities by **finish time**.
- Select the first activity (the one that finishes the earliest).
- For each subsequent activity, select it if its start time is after the finish time of the previously selected activity.

This approach works because by selecting the activity that finishes the earliest, we leave the most room for the remaining activities.

Example: Given activities with start and finish times:

```sql

Start    Finish
1        3
2        5
4        6
6        8
5        7
3        9
```

The greedy approach selects:

1. Activity (1, 3)
2. Activity (4, 6)
3. Activity (6, 8)

Thus, the maximum number of non-overlapping activities is 3.

C++ Code for Activity Selection using Greedy Algorithm:

```cpp

#include <iostream>
#include <vector>
#include <algorithm>
using namespace std;

struct Activity {
    int start;
    int finish;
```

201

```cpp
};

bool compare(Activity a, Activity b) {
    return a.finish < b.finish;    // Sort by finish time
}

int activitySelection(vector<Activity>& activities) {
    sort(activities.begin(), activities.end(), compare);

    int count = 1;   // Always select the first activity
    int lastFinishTime = activities[0].finish;

    for (int i = 1; i < activities.size(); i++) {
        if (activities[i].start >= lastFinishTime) {
            count++;   // Select the activity
            lastFinishTime = activities[i].finish;   // Update the last finish time
        }
    }

    return count;
}
```

```
int main() {
    vector<Activity> activities = {
        {1, 3}, {2, 5}, {4, 6}, {6, 8}, {5, 7},
{3, 9}
    };

    cout << "Maximum number of activities: " <<
activitySelection(activities) << endl;

    return 0;
}
```

Time Complexity: O(n log n) due to the sorting step, where n is the number of activities. The greedy part (iterating through the activities) has a time complexity of O(n).

When to Use Greedy Algorithms

Greedy algorithms are effective for problems where:

- The **greedy-choice property** holds, meaning making a local optimal choice leads to a globally optimal solution.
- The problem has **optimal substructure**, meaning the optimal solution to the problem can be built from optimal solutions to its subproblems.

Examples of problems that can be solved using greedy algorithms include:

- **Huffman coding** for data compression.
- **Minimum spanning tree** (e.g., Kruskal's or Prim's algorithm).
- **Dijkstra's shortest path algorithm** for finding the shortest path in a graph.

However, greedy algorithms do not always guarantee an optimal solution for all problems. In cases where the problem does not exhibit the greedy-choice property or optimal substructure, more complex algorithms such as **dynamic programming** or **backtracking** may be more appropriate.

Summary of Key Concepts:

- **Greedy Algorithms**: Algorithms that make locally optimal choices at each step with the hope of finding a globally optimal solution.
- **Greedy-Choice Property**: A property that ensures making the best local choice leads to a globally optimal solution.
- **Optimal Substructure**: A property that ensures the optimal solution to a problem can be constructed from optimal solutions to its subproblems.
- **Real-World Examples**: The **coin change problem, activity selection problem, Huffman coding**, and **minimum spanning tree** can all be solved using greedy algorithms.

- **Limitations**: Greedy algorithms may not always produce optimal solutions for problems that do not have the greedy-choice property.

Greedy algorithms are often efficient and easy to implement, making them ideal for certain types of problems where the problem structure fits well with the greedy approach. Let me know if you'd like more examples or a deeper explanation on any of these topics!

CHAPTER 19

DIVIDE AND CONQUER ALGORITHMS

In this chapter, we will delve into **divide and conquer** algorithms, a powerful paradigm for solving complex problems. We will explore how divide and conquer works, examine some common problems solved using this approach (such as **merge sort** and **quicksort**), and discuss how to optimize algorithms using divide and conquer.

Introduction to Divide and Conquer

Divide and conquer is an algorithmic paradigm that breaks a problem down into smaller subproblems, solves each subproblem independently, and combines the results to form the final solution. This technique is widely used for problems that can be recursively divided into smaller instances of the same problem.

The main idea behind divide and conquer is:

1. **Divide**: Split the problem into smaller subproblems that are easier to solve.
2. **Conquer**: Solve the subproblems independently, usually recursively.

3. **Combine**: Combine the solutions of the subproblems to form the final solution.

This approach is effective because solving smaller problems is often more manageable, and the solutions to these smaller problems can be combined in a systematic way.

Key Characteristics of Divide and Conquer Algorithms:

- **Recursion**: Most divide and conquer algorithms are recursive, meaning they solve smaller subproblems and build up to the solution.
- **Efficiency**: Many divide and conquer algorithms reduce time complexity by breaking problems into smaller subproblems and solving them more efficiently.
- **Optimal Substructure**: Like dynamic programming, divide and conquer problems often have optimal substructure, meaning the solution to the problem can be constructed from solutions to its subproblems.

Example Problems Solved with Divide and Conquer

Let's look at a few classic problems that can be solved efficiently using the divide and conquer technique.

1. Merge Sort

Merge sort is one of the most famous divide and conquer algorithms. It recursively divides the input array into two halves, sorts each half, and then merges the sorted halves back together.

Merge Sort Algorithm:

1. **Divide**: Split the array into two halves.
2. **Conquer**: Recursively sort each half.
3. **Combine**: Merge the two sorted halves to produce the sorted array.

C++ Code for Merge Sort:

cpp

```
#include <iostream>
#include <vector>
using namespace std;

void merge(vector<int>& arr, int left, int mid,
int right) {
    int n1 = mid - left + 1;
    int n2 = right - mid;

    vector<int> L(n1), R(n2);
```

```
    for (int i = 0; i < n1; i++) L[i] = arr[left
+ i];
    for (int i = 0; i < n2; i++) R[i] = arr[mid
+ 1 + i];

    int i = 0, j = 0, k = left;
    while (i < n1 && j < n2) {
        if (L[i] <= R[j]) {
            arr[k] = L[i];
            i++;
        } else {
            arr[k] = R[j];
            j++;
        }
        k++;
    }

    while (i < n1) {
        arr[k] = L[i];
        i++;
        k++;
    }

    while (j < n2) {
        arr[k] = R[j];
        j++;
        k++;
    }
}
```

```cpp
void mergeSort(vector<int>& arr, int left, int
right) {
    if (left < right) {
        int mid = left + (right - left) / 2;

        mergeSort(arr, left, mid);                //
Recursively sort the left half
        mergeSort(arr, mid + 1, right);    //
Recursively sort the right half

        merge(arr, left, mid, right);    // Merge
the sorted halves
    }
}

int main() {
    vector<int> arr = {12, 11, 13, 5, 6, 7};
    int n = arr.size();

    mergeSort(arr, 0, n - 1);

    cout << "Sorted array: ";
    for (int num : arr) {
        cout << num << " ";
    }
    cout << endl;

    return 0;
```

}

Time Complexity: O(n log n) for both average and worst-case scenarios.

- **Divide** step takes O(log n) time (due to recursive division).
- **Conquer** step takes O(n) time (due to merging). Thus, the overall time complexity is O(n log n).

2. Quick Sort

Quick sort is another popular divide and conquer algorithm that partitions the array around a pivot element and recursively sorts the subarrays on either side of the pivot.

Quick Sort Algorithm:

1. **Divide**: Choose a pivot element, then partition the array such that all elements less than the pivot are on one side, and all elements greater than the pivot are on the other side.
2. **Conquer**: Recursively sort the left and right subarrays.
3. **Combine**: Since the array is sorted in place, no merging is needed.

C++ Code for Quick Sort:

cpp

```cpp
#include <iostream>
using namespace std;

int partition(int arr[], int low, int high) {
    int pivot = arr[high];  // Choosing the last
element as the pivot
    int i = low - 1;

    for (int j = low; j < high; j++) {
        if (arr[j] < pivot) {
            i++;
            swap(arr[i], arr[j]);
        }
    }
    swap(arr[i + 1], arr[high]);
    return i + 1;
}


void quickSort(int arr[], int low, int high) {
    if (low < high) {
        int pi = partition(arr, low, high);  //
Partitioning index
        quickSort(arr, low, pi - 1);    //
Recursively sort the left part
        quickSort(arr, pi + 1, high);    //
Recursively sort the right part
    }
}
```

```
int main() {
    int arr[] = {10, 7, 8, 9, 1, 5};
    int n = sizeof(arr) / sizeof(arr[0]);

    quickSort(arr, 0, n - 1);

    cout << "Sorted array: ";
    for (int i = 0; i < n; i++) {
        cout << arr[i] << " ";
    }
    cout << endl;

    return 0;
}
```

Time Complexity:

- **Best and Average Case**: O(n log n), where the pivot divides the array evenly.
- **Worst Case**: O(n²) when the pivot is poorly chosen (e.g., always the smallest or largest element).

3. Optimizing with Divide and Conquer

Divide and conquer algorithms often optimize the performance of traditional algorithms by reducing the problem size at each step, leading to faster solutions for large problems. The following strategies can help optimize divide and conquer algorithms:

213

1. **Efficient Partitioning**: Choosing an efficient pivot (in quicksort) or a good way to split the problem (in merge sort) can significantly improve performance.

2. **Avoiding Redundant Work**: In algorithms like **matrix multiplication** or **Strassen's algorithm**, using divide and conquer can reduce the overall computational complexity by avoiding redundant calculations.

3. **Optimized Data Structures**: Implementing divide and conquer algorithms with efficient data structures (e.g., using linked lists for merge sort) can further improve time and space complexity.

Real-World Problems Solved with Divide and Conquer

Divide and conquer algorithms are used in a wide variety of real-world applications, especially when dealing with large datasets or problems that require repetitive subproblems to be solved efficiently.

1. Fast Fourier Transform (FFT)

FFT is an algorithm to compute the **discrete Fourier transform (DFT)** and its inverse efficiently. This is widely used in signal processing, image compression (JPEG), and audio processing. FFT uses a divide and conquer approach to divide the problem into smaller subproblems and combine their results efficiently.

2. Matrix Multiplication

Matrix multiplication is an example where divide and conquer can significantly reduce the complexity. Strassen's algorithm is a divide and conquer algorithm that multiplies matrices faster than the standard $O(n^3)$ algorithm.

3. Closest Pair of Points

The **closest pair of points** problem is a classic example where divide and conquer is used to find the two closest points in a set of points in the plane. The problem is solved by dividing the points into two halves, recursively finding the closest pairs in each half, and then combining the results to find the closest pair across the divide.

4. Binary Search

Though binary search is typically considered a simple algorithm, it is a fundamental example of divide and conquer. It efficiently finds an element in a sorted array by dividing the array in half at each step.

Summary of Key Concepts:

- **Divide and Conquer**: A paradigm where problems are broken down into smaller subproblems that are solved independently and then combined to solve the overall problem.

- **Merge Sort**: A divide and conquer algorithm with a time complexity of O(n log n) that divides the array into two halves, sorts each half, and merges them.
- **Quick Sort**: A divide and conquer algorithm that uses a pivot element to partition the array and recursively sorts the subarrays.
- **Optimization**: Divide and conquer helps optimize algorithms by reducing problem size at each step, leading to faster solutions for large problems.
- **Real-World Applications**: Divide and conquer is used in applications such as FFT, matrix multiplication, and the closest pair of points problem.

Divide and conquer is a fundamental technique for solving complex problems efficiently. It reduces computational complexity and is essential for handling large datasets in many domains. Let me know if you'd like more examples or further details on any of these concepts!

CHAPTER 20

BACKTRACKING ALGORITHMS

In this chapter, we will explore **backtracking algorithms**, a powerful problem-solving technique used to find solutions to problems that involve making a series of choices. Backtracking is particularly useful for problems where the solution space is large and consists of possible choices that must be systematically explored. We will also cover **example problems** such as the **N-Queens problem** and the **subset sum problem**, and demonstrate how to implement backtracking in C++.

What is Backtracking?

Backtracking is a general algorithm for finding solutions to problems by trying partial solutions and then abandoning them if they are determined to not lead to a valid solution. The algorithm explores all possible solutions by **building a solution incrementally** and then **backtracking** when a partial solution is found to be invalid.

The basic idea of backtracking is:

1. **Choose**: Pick a choice that seems promising.
2. **Explore**: Recursively explore the subsequent choices.

3. **Backtrack**: If a choice leads to a solution that doesn't work (i.e., violates the constraints or doesn't meet the requirements), undo the choice and try a different one.

Backtracking is essentially **depth-first search (DFS)**, but with the addition of undoing (or "backtracking") when you reach an invalid or incomplete solution.

Key Steps in Backtracking:

1. **Choice**: At each step, choose one possibility from the available options.
2. **Constraints**: Check whether the chosen option is valid or violates any constraints.
3. **Goal**: If the current state meets the goal, record the solution.
4. **Backtrack**: If a valid solution isn't found, undo the previous choice (backtrack) and explore the next possible option.

Example Problems Solved with Backtracking

1. N-Queens Problem

The **N-Queens problem** is a classic backtracking problem that asks for all possible arrangements of N queens on an N x N chessboard such that no two queens threaten each other. A queen can attack another queen if they are in the same row, column, or diagonal.

Approach:

- Place one queen in each row, ensuring no two queens share the same column or diagonal.
- Use backtracking to explore all possible configurations, and when an invalid position is reached (i.e., queens attack each other), backtrack to try a different configuration.

C++ Code for N-Queens Problem:

cpp

```cpp
#include <iostream>
#include <vector>
using namespace std;

bool isSafe(int board[], int row, int col) {
    // Check previous columns in the current row
    for (int i = 0; i < col; i++) {
        if (board[i] == row || abs(board[i] -
row) == abs(i - col)) {
            return false;
        }
    }
    return true;
```

```cpp
}


bool solveNQueens(int board[], int col, int N) {
    if (col >= N) {
        // All queens are placed
        for (int i = 0; i < N; i++) {
            for (int j = 0; j < N; j++) {
                if (board[i] == j)
                    cout << "Q ";
                else
                    cout << ". ";
            }
            cout << endl;
        }
        cout << endl;
        return true;   // Found a valid solution
    }

    bool res = false;
    for (int row = 0; row < N; row++) {
        if (isSafe(board, row, col)) {
            board[col] = row;
            res = solveNQueens(board, col + 1, N)
|| res; // Explore next column
            board[col] = -1;   // Backtrack
        }
    }
    return res;
}
```

```
int main() {
    int N = 4;   // Number of queens
    int board[N];
    fill(board, board + N, -1); // Initialize the
board

    solveNQueens(board, 0, N);

    return 0;
}
```

Explanation:

- **isSafe** function checks if placing a queen in a particular position is valid (i.e., no conflict with already placed queens).
- The **solveNQueens** function places queens one by one, column by column, and uses backtracking to try different rows when a conflict occurs.

Time Complexity: The worst-case time complexity of this algorithm is O(N!), as there are N rows to place queens, and each placement has N possibilities, leading to N! possible configurations.

2. Subset Sum Problem

The **subset sum problem** is a problem in which, given a set of integers and a target sum, you need to determine whether there is a subset of the integers that sums up to the target sum.

Approach:

- Try all possible subsets by including or excluding each number, using backtracking.
- If a subset sum matches the target, return true. Otherwise, backtrack and try other subsets.

C++ Code for Subset Sum Problem:

cpp

```cpp
#include <iostream>
#include <vector>
using namespace std;

bool isSubsetSum(vector<int>& arr, int target,
int index) {
    // Base cases
    if (target == 0) return true;   // Found a
valid subset
    if (index == 0) return arr[0] == target;   //
Only one element left to check
```

```cpp
    // If we exclude the current element
    if (isSubsetSum(arr, target, index - 1))
return true;

    // If we include the current element
    if (arr[index] <= target && isSubsetSum(arr,
target - arr[index], index - 1)) return true;

    return false;
}

int main() {
    vector<int> arr = {3, 34, 4, 12, 5, 2};  //
Given set
    int target = 9;  // Target sum
    int n = arr.size();

    if (isSubsetSum(arr, target, n - 1))
        cout << "Subset with sum " << target <<
" exists." << endl;
    else
        cout << "Subset with sum " << target <<
" does not exist." << endl;

    return 0;
}
```

Explanation:

- **isSubsetSum** recursively checks if a subset of the array sums up to the target. At each step, we have the option to either include or exclude the current element in the subset.
- We explore all possible subsets using backtracking.

Time Complexity: $O(2^n)$, as the algorithm explores all subsets of the array.

How to Implement Backtracking in C++

Backtracking algorithms are typically implemented using **recursion**. Here are the key steps to implement a backtracking solution in C++:

1. **Recursive Function**: Create a function that explores the decision space (i.e., tries different solutions).
2. **Base Case**: Define the base case(s) where the recursion terminates. This is usually when the solution is found or when no further choices can be made.
3. **Choices**: At each level of recursion, try all possible choices (usually involving decision-making and state changes).
4. **Backtrack**: After each choice, either accept the solution or undo the last change (i.e., backtrack) to explore other options.

Example Framework for Backtracking:

cpp

```cpp
#include <iostream>
#include <vector>
using namespace std;

void backtrack(vector<int>& solution, int n, int k) {
    // Base case: solution is valid, print it
    if (solution.size() == k) {
        for (int i : solution) cout << i << " ";
        cout << endl;
        return;
    }

    // Explore further choices
    for (int i = 1; i <= n; i++) {
        solution.push_back(i);  // Choose
        backtrack(solution, n, k);  // Recurse
        solution.pop_back();   // Undo choice (backtrack)
    }
}

int main() {
    int n = 3;  // Number of items
    int k = 2;  // Size of the subset
    vector<int> solution;
    backtrack(solution, n, k);
```

```
    return 0;
}
```

In this framework:

- The **base case** is when the solution has reached the required size k.
- The **choices** are represented by trying different numbers in each recursion.
- After exploring one choice, the algorithm **backtracks** by removing the last number and trying a new one.

Summary of Key Concepts:

- **Backtracking** is a recursive algorithmic technique that involves trying possible solutions incrementally and undoing (backtracking) when a solution is invalid or incomplete.
- **N-Queens Problem**: A classic backtracking problem where we place queens on a chessboard such that no two queens attack each other.
- **Subset Sum Problem**: A problem where we determine if a subset of numbers from a set adds up to a given target sum.
- **Backtracking Implementation**: Implemented recursively, backtracking algorithms explore all

possibilities, backtrack on invalid choices, and build up solutions incrementally.

Backtracking is a versatile technique used for solving combinatorial problems where the solution involves choosing or rejecting candidates at each step. It's particularly useful for optimization problems, constraint satisfaction problems, and puzzles. Let me know if you'd like more examples or further explanations!

CHAPTER 21

GRAPH ALGORITHMS

In this chapter, we will cover several important **graph algorithms** that are widely used in computer science and real-world applications. These algorithms include **shortest path algorithms** (Dijkstra and Bellman-Ford), **minimum spanning tree algorithms** (Kruskal's and Prim's), and **topological sorting** and **cycle detection**. Graphs are powerful tools for modeling relationships in many applications, from network routing to scheduling problems.

Shortest Path Algorithms: Dijkstra and Bellman-Ford

Shortest path algorithms are used to find the shortest path between two nodes in a graph, which is useful in many applications such as routing, network flow, and GPS navigation systems.

1. Dijkstra's Algorithm

Dijkstra's algorithm is used to find the shortest path from a source node to all other nodes in a **weighted graph**. It works for graphs with non-negative edge weights.

Key Features:

- It is a **greedy algorithm** that always picks the closest node to the source node.
- It uses a **priority queue** (min-heap) to select the node with the smallest tentative distance.

Algorithm Steps:

1. Initialize the distance to the source node as 0 and all other nodes as infinity.
2. Use a priority queue to explore nodes with the smallest tentative distance.
3. For each node, update the tentative distance of its neighbors based on the edge weights.
4. Repeat until all nodes have been visited.

C++ Code for Dijkstra's Algorithm:

cpp

```
#include <iostream>
#include <vector>
#include <queue>
#include <climits>
using namespace std;

typedef pair<int, int> pii;  // {distance, node}

void  dijkstra(vector<vector<pii>>&  adj,  int
source, int V) {
```

```cpp
    vector<int> dist(V, INT_MAX);    // Distance
array
    dist[source] = 0;

    priority_queue<pii,               vector<pii>,
greater<pii>> pq;  // Min-heap priority queue
    pq.push({0, source});

    while (!pq.empty()) {
        int u = pq.top().second;
        int d = pq.top().first;
        pq.pop();

        if (d > dist[u]) continue;  // Skip if a
better distance has already been found

        for (auto& neighbor : adj[u]) {
            int v = neighbor.first;
            int weight = neighbor.second;

            if (dist[u] + weight < dist[v]) {
                dist[v] = dist[u] + weight;
                pq.push({dist[v], v});
            }
        }
    }

    // Print the shortest distances
    for (int i = 0; i < V; i++) {
```

```cpp
        if (dist[i] == INT_MAX) {
            cout << "Node " << i << " is
unreachable from source" << endl;
        } else {
            cout << "Distance from source to node
" << i << ": " << dist[i] << endl;
        }
    }
}


int main() {
    int V = 5;   // Number of vertices
    vector<vector<pii>> adj(V);

    adj[0].push_back({1, 10});
    adj[0].push_back({4, 5});
    adj[1].push_back({2, 1});
    adj[2].push_back({3, 4});
    adj[3].push_back({0, 7});
    adj[4].push_back({1, 3});
    adj[4].push_back({2, 9});

    int source = 0;   // Starting node
    dijkstra(adj, source, V);

    return 0;
}
```

Time Complexity: O(E log V), where E is the number of edges and V is the number of vertices. This is due to the use of a priority queue (min-heap) for extracting the node with the smallest tentative distance.

2. Bellman-Ford Algorithm

Bellman-Ford's algorithm is another shortest path algorithm that works for graphs with negative edge weights. Unlike Dijkstra's algorithm, it can handle negative weights and even detect negative weight cycles.

Key Features:

- It can handle graphs with **negative weight edges**.
- It works by **relaxing** all edges repeatedly, which is a process of updating the distance to a vertex if a shorter path is found.

Algorithm Steps:

1. Initialize the distance to the source node as 0 and all other nodes as infinity.
2. For each edge in the graph, if the distance to a vertex can be reduced by taking the edge, update the distance.
3. Repeat this process **V-1** times (where V is the number of vertices).

4. Check for negative weight cycles by attempting to relax the edges one more time.

C++ Code for Bellman-Ford Algorithm:

cpp

```cpp
#include <iostream>
#include <vector>
#include <climits>
using namespace std;

struct Edge {
    int u, v, weight;
};

bool bellmanFord(int V, vector<Edge>& edges, int source) {
    vector<int> dist(V, INT_MAX);
    dist[source] = 0;

    for (int i = 1; i < V; i++) {
        for (auto& edge : edges) {
            if (dist[edge.u] != INT_MAX && dist[edge.u] + edge.weight < dist[edge.v]) {
                dist[edge.v] = dist[edge.u] + edge.weight;
            }
        }
```

```cpp
    }

    // Check for negative weight cycles
    for (auto& edge : edges) {
        if (dist[edge.u] != INT_MAX &&
dist[edge.u] + edge.weight < dist[edge.v]) {
            cout << "Graph contains a negative
weight cycle!" << endl;
            return false;
        }
    }

    // Print shortest distances
    for (int i = 0; i < V; i++) {
        if (dist[i] == INT_MAX) {
            cout << "Node " << i << " is
unreachable from source" << endl;
        } else {
            cout << "Distance from source to node
" << i << ": " << dist[i] << endl;
        }
    }
    return true;
}

int main() {
    int V = 5;  // Number of vertices
    vector<Edge> edges = {
        {0, 1, -1}, {0, 2, 4},
```

234

```
        {1, 2, 3}, {1, 3, 2}, {1, 4, 2},
        {3, 1, 1}, {3, 2, 5},
        {4, 3, -3}
    };

    int source = 0;
    bellmanFord(V, edges, source);

    return 0;
}
```

Time Complexity: O(V * E), where V is the number of vertices and E is the number of edges. The algorithm performs V-1 iterations over all the edges, and each iteration takes O(E) time.

Minimum Spanning Tree (MST) Algorithms: Kruskal's and Prim's

A **minimum spanning tree (MST)** of a connected, undirected graph is a tree that connects all the vertices in the graph with the minimum possible total edge weight.

1. Kruskal's Algorithm

Kruskal's algorithm is a greedy algorithm used to find the MST by selecting edges with the smallest weights and adding them to the MST, ensuring no cycles are formed.

Algorithm Steps:

1. Sort all the edges of the graph by their weights.

2. Initialize a forest (a set of trees) where each vertex is in its own tree.

3. Iterate over the edges, and for each edge:

    o If the edge connects two different trees, add it to the MST.

    o If it forms a cycle (both vertices are in the same tree), discard the edge.

4. Repeat until all vertices are connected.

C++ Code for Kruskal's Algorithm:

cpp

```
#include <iostream>
#include <vector>
#include <algorithm>
using namespace std;

struct Edge {
    int u, v, weight;
};

class DisjointSet {
public:
    vector<int> parent, rank;

    DisjointSet(int n) {
        parent.resize(n);
```

```cpp
        rank.resize(n, 0);
        for (int i = 0; i < n; i++) parent[i] =
i;
    }

    int find(int u) {
        if (u != parent[u])
            parent[u] = find(parent[u]);  // Path
compression
        return parent[u];
    }

    void unite(int u, int v) {
        int root_u = find(u);
        int root_v = find(v);
        if (root_u != root_v) {
            if (rank[root_u] > rank[root_v]) {
                parent[root_v] = root_u;
            } else  if  (rank[root_u]   <
rank[root_v]) {
                parent[root_u] = root_v;
            } else {
                parent[root_v] = root_u;
                rank[root_u]++;
            }
        }
    }
};
```

```cpp
void kruskal(int V, vector<Edge>& edges) {
    DisjointSet ds(V);

    // Sort edges by weight
    sort(edges.begin(), edges.end(), [](Edge a,
Edge b) {
        return a.weight < b.weight;
    });

    int mstWeight = 0;
    for (Edge& edge : edges) {
        int u = edge.u;
        int v = edge.v;
        int weight = edge.weight;

        if (ds.find(u) != ds.find(v)) {
            ds.unite(u, v);
            mstWeight += weight;
            cout << "Edge (" << u << ", " << v <<
") with weight " << weight << " added to MST" <<
endl;
        }
    }

    cout << "Total weight of MST: " << mstWeight
<< endl;
}

int main() {
```

```
int V = 4;   // Number of vertices
vector<Edge> edges = {
    {0, 1, 10}, {0, 2, 6}, {0, 3, 5},
    {1, 3, 15}, {2, 3, 4}
};

kruskal(V, edges);

return 0;
}
```

Time Complexity: O(E log E), where E is the number of edges. Sorting the edges takes O(E log E), and the union-find operations take nearly constant time due to path compression and union by rank.

2. Prim's Algorithm

Prim's algorithm is another greedy algorithm for finding the MST, but instead of sorting edges like Kruskal's, it starts from an arbitrary node and grows the MST by adding the minimum weight edge that connects a vertex in the MST to a vertex outside the MST.

Algorithm Steps:

1. Start with an arbitrary vertex and mark it as part of the MST.

2. At each step, select the edge with the minimum weight that connects a vertex in the MST to a vertex outside the MST.

3. Repeat until all vertices are included in the MST.

C++ Code for Prim's Algorithm:

cpp

```cpp
#include <iostream>
#include <vector>
#include <queue>
#include <climits>
using namespace std;

void prim(int V, vector<vector<pair<int, int>>>&
adj) {
    vector<int> key(V, INT_MAX);
    vector<bool> inMST(V, false);
    priority_queue<pair<int,                  int>,
vector<pair<int, int>>, greater<pair<int, int>>>
pq;

    pq.push({0, 0});   // {key, vertex}
    key[0] = 0;

    int mstWeight = 0;
    while (!pq.empty()) {
        int u = pq.top().second;
```

```cpp
        pq.pop();

        if (inMST[u]) continue;
        inMST[u] = true;
        mstWeight += key[u];

        for (auto& neighbor : adj[u]) {
            int v = neighbor.first;
            int weight = neighbor.second;
            if (!inMST[v] && weight < key[v]) {
                key[v] = weight;
                pq.push({key[v], v});
            }
        }
    }

    cout << "Total weight of MST: " << mstWeight
<< endl;
}

int main() {
    int V = 5;   // Number of vertices
    vector<vector<pair<int, int>>> adj(V);

    adj[0].push_back({1, 2});
    adj[0].push_back({3, 6});
    adj[1].push_back({0, 2});
    adj[1].push_back({2, 3});
    adj[2].push_back({1, 3});
```

```
adj[2].push_back({3, 8});
adj[3].push_back({0, 6});
adj[3].push_back({2, 8});
adj[3].push_back({4, 9});
adj[4].push_back({3, 9});

prim(V, adj);

return 0;
}
```

Time Complexity: O(E log V), where E is the number of edges and V is the number of vertices. The priority queue is updated for each edge.

Topological Sorting and Cycle Detection

1. Topological Sorting

Topological sorting is an algorithm for ordering the vertices of a Directed Acyclic Graph (DAG) such that for every directed edge (u, v), vertex u comes before v in the ordering.

Algorithm Steps:

1. Find a vertex with no incoming edges (in-degree 0) and add it to the topological order.
2. Remove this vertex from the graph and repeat until all vertices are processed.

C++ Code for Topological Sort:

cpp

```cpp
#include <iostream>
#include <vector>
#include <stack>
#include <queue>
using namespace std;

void topologicalSort(int V, vector<vector<int>>&
adj) {
    vector<int> inDegree(V, 0);

    for (int i = 0; i < V; i++) {
        for (int v : adj[i]) {
            inDegree[v]++;
        }
    }

    queue<int> q;
    for (int i = 0; i < V; i++) {
        if (inDegree[i] == 0) q.push(i);
    }

    vector<int> topoOrder;
    while (!q.empty()) {
        int u = q.front();
        q.pop();
        topoOrder.push_back(u);
```

```cpp
        for (int v : adj[u]) {
            if (--inDegree[v] == 0) q.push(v);
        }
    }

    if (topoOrder.size() != V) {
        cout << "The graph has a cycle,
topological sorting is not possible." << endl;
        return;
    }

    cout << "Topological Sort: ";
    for (int v : topoOrder) {
        cout << v << " ";
    }
    cout << endl;
}

int main() {
    int V = 6;
    vector<vector<int>> adj(V);

    adj[5].push_back(2);
    adj[5].push_back(0);
    adj[4].push_back(0);
    adj[4].push_back(1);
    adj[2].push_back(3);
    adj[3].push_back(1);
```

```
    topologicalSort(V, adj);

    return 0;
}
```

2. Cycle Detection

Cycle detection in a directed graph can be done using topological sorting. If a graph contains a cycle, then it is not possible to sort the vertices topologically. This can be detected when the number of vertices in the topological order is less than the total number of vertices in the graph.

C++ Code for Cycle Detection:

cpp

```cpp
#include <iostream>
#include <vector>
#include <queue>
using namespace std;

bool hasCycle(int V, vector<vector<int>>& adj) {
    vector<int> inDegree(V, 0);

    for (int i = 0; i < V; i++) {
        for (int v : adj[i]) {
            inDegree[v]++;
        }
```

```cpp
    }

    queue<int> q;
    for (int i = 0; i < V; i++) {
        if (inDegree[i] == 0) q.push(i);
    }

    int count = 0;
    while (!q.empty()) {
        int u = q.front();
        q.pop();
        count++;

        for (int v : adj[u]) {
            if (--inDegree[v] == 0) q.push(v);
        }
    }

    return count != V;   // If count is less than
V, the graph has a cycle
}

int main() {
    int V = 6;
    vector<vector<int>> adj(V);

    adj[5].push_back(2);
    adj[5].push_back(0);
    adj[4].push_back(0);
```

```
adj[4].push_back(1);
adj[2].push_back(3);
adj[3].push_back(1);

if (hasCycle(V, adj)) {
    cout << "The graph has a cycle." << endl;
} else {
    cout << "The graph has no cycle." <<
endl;
}

return 0;
}
```

Summary of Key Concepts:

- **Shortest Path Algorithms**: **Dijkstra's** is efficient for graphs with non-negative weights, while **Bellman-Ford** handles graphs with negative weights and detects negative cycles.

- **Minimum Spanning Tree**: **Kruskal's** and **Prim's** algorithms are used to find the minimum spanning tree in a graph, with different approaches for edge selection.

- **Topological Sorting**: Used for **directed acyclic graphs (DAGs)** to order vertices such that for every edge (u, v), u comes before v.

- **Cycle Detection**: Topological sorting can also detect cycles in directed graphs, as a cycle prevents a valid topological sort.

These algorithms are fundamental for graph-related problems and have numerous applications in networking, scheduling, and optimization problems. Let me know if you need more examples or further explanations!

CHAPTER 22

ADVANCED DATA STRUCTURES: SUFFIX ARRAYS, SEGMENT TREES, AND FENWICK TREES

In this chapter, we will explore three advanced data structures that are used for solving complex problems in an efficient manner: **suffix arrays**, **segment trees**, and **Fenwick trees** (also known as **binary indexed trees**). These data structures are crucial for tackling problems related to string processing, range queries, and dynamic updates, making them essential in many fields, such as competitive programming, text processing, and real-time systems.

Introduction to Advanced Data Structures

Advanced data structures are essential for optimizing algorithm performance when dealing with large datasets, particularly for problems that require efficient updates, queries, or both. While basic data structures like arrays, linked lists, and hash tables can be sufficient for many tasks, more complex problems often require specialized structures for efficiency.

- **Suffix Arrays**: A data structure used in string processing problems that efficiently stores and manages suffixes of a string.
- **Segment Trees**: A tree-like data structure used for efficient range queries and updates on arrays, especially for problems like range minimum/maximum, sum, and other operations.
- **Fenwick Trees (Binary Indexed Trees)**: A data structure that provides efficient methods for cumulative frequency table operations, such as prefix sums and range queries.

These data structures allow for optimized performance in both time and space, especially for problems involving large datasets or requiring frequent updates and queries.

Segment Trees

A **segment tree** is a binary tree data structure used for efficient range queries and updates. It is particularly useful for problems where you need to compute values over a segment (or subarray) of an array, such as sum, minimum, or maximum, in **O(log n)** time.

Key Features:

- **Range Queries**: Segment trees allow you to query a range of values (e.g., the sum of elements between indices i and j) efficiently.
- **Point Updates**: Segment trees support efficient updates to individual elements in the array, allowing changes in **O(log n)** time.
- **Space Complexity**: A segment tree requires **O(n)** space, where n is the size of the array.

Segment Tree Example: Range Sum Query

Let's consider an example where we want to compute the **sum** of elements in a given range [L, R] of an array. We will build a segment tree to efficiently handle such queries.

C++ Code for Segment Tree:

cpp

```cpp
#include <iostream>
#include <vector>
using namespace std;

class SegmentTree {
private:
    vector<int> tree;
```

```cpp
int n;

void build(const vector<int>& arr, int node,
int start, int end) {
    if (start == end) {
        tree[node] = arr[start];    // Leaf
node holds the element
    } else {
        int mid = (start + end) / 2;
        build(arr,   2*node,   start,   mid);
// Left child
        build(arr, 2*node + 1, mid + 1, end);
// Right child
        tree[node]   =   tree[2*node]   +
tree[2*node + 1];  // Internal node holds the sum
of its children
    }
}

int query(int node, int start, int end, int
L, int R) {
    if (R < start || end < L) {
        return 0;  // Out of range
    }
    if (L <= start && end <= R) {
        return tree[node];  // Fully within
range
    }
    int mid = (start + end) / 2;
```

```cpp
        int leftQuery = query(2*node, start, mid,
L, R);        // Query left child
        int rightQuery = query(2*node + 1, mid +
1, end, L, R);  // Query right child
        return leftQuery + rightQuery;
    }


    void update(int node, int start, int end, int
idx, int val) {
        if (start == end) {
            tree[node] = val;   // Update the leaf
node
        } else {
            int mid = (start + end) / 2;
            if (start <= idx && idx <= mid) {
                update(2*node, start, mid, idx,
val);   // Update in the left child
            } else {
                update(2*node + 1, mid + 1, end,
idx, val);   // Update in the right child
            }
            tree[node]    =    tree[2*node]    +
tree[2*node + 1];   // Recompute the value for the
internal node
        }
    }

public:
    SegmentTree(const vector<int>& arr) {
```

253

```cpp
        n = arr.size();
        tree.resize(4 * n);   // Allocate space
for the segment tree
        build(arr, 1, 0, n - 1);   // Build the
tree
    }

    int query(int L, int R) {
        return query(1, 0, n - 1, L, R);   // Call
query on the root node
    }

    void update(int idx, int val) {
        update(1, 0, n - 1, idx, val);   // Call
update on the root node
    }
};

int main() {
    vector<int> arr = {1, 3, 5, 7, 9, 11};
    SegmentTree segTree(arr);

    cout << "Sum of values in range [1, 3]: " <<
segTree.query(1, 3) << endl;   // Output: 15

    segTree.update(1, 10);   // Update element at
index 1 to 10
```

```
    cout << "Sum of values in range [1, 3] after
update: " << segTree.query(1, 3) << endl;   //
Output: 22


    return 0;
}
```

Time Complexity:

- **Build**: O(n), where n is the size of the input array.
- **Query**: O(log n) for a range query.
- **Update**: O(log n) for updating an element in the array.

Applications of Segment Trees:

- Range sum queries.
- Range minimum/maximum queries.
- Range updates (with some modifications).

Fenwick Trees (Binary Indexed Trees)

A **Fenwick Tree** (also called a **binary indexed tree**, or **BIT**) is a data structure that efficiently supports cumulative frequency tables, allowing for **O(log n)** time complexity for both point updates and range queries. Fenwick trees are particularly useful for problems that involve dynamic frequency counts or cumulative sums.

255

Key Features:

- **Point Updates**: Modify a single element and update the tree in logarithmic time.
- **Prefix Sum Queries**: Compute the sum of elements from the start of the array to a given index in logarithmic time.
- **Space Complexity**: $O(n)$, where n is the size of the array.

Fenwick Tree Example: Prefix Sum Query

Let's consider the problem of calculating the **prefix sum** of an array using a Fenwick Tree. A prefix sum is the sum of all elements from index 0 to index i.

C++ Code for Fenwick Tree:

```cpp
#include <iostream>
#include <vector>
using namespace std;

class FenwickTree {
private:
    vector<int> BITree;
    int n;

    int lsb(int i) {
```

```cpp
        return  i  &  (-i);      // Get  least
significant bit
    }

public:
    FenwickTree(int size) {
        n = size;
        BITree.resize(n + 1, 0);   // Initialize
Fenwick Tree with 0s
    }

    void update(int index, int value) {
        while (index <= n) {
            BITree[index] += value;   // Update
the value at the index
            index += lsb(index);   // Move to the
next index to update
        }
    }

    int query(int index) {
        int sum = 0;
        while (index > 0) {
            sum += BITree[index];   // Add the
value at the index
            index -= lsb(index);   // Move to the
parent index
        }
        return sum;
```

257

```
    }
};

int main() {
    FenwickTree fenwick(6);

    // Perform updates
    fenwick.update(1, 3);
    fenwick.update(2, 5);
    fenwick.update(3, 7);

    cout << "Prefix sum up to index 3: " <<
fenwick.query(3) << endl;   // Output: 15
    cout << "Prefix sum up to index 2: " <<
fenwick.query(2) << endl;   // Output: 8

    return 0;
}
```

Time Complexity:

- **Update**: O(log n).
- **Query**: O(log n).

Applications of Fenwick Trees:

- Prefix sum queries.
- Dynamic frequency counting (e.g., count of numbers in a range).

- Range sum queries with updates.

Applications and Optimization

- **Text Searching**: Suffix arrays are used for efficient string matching and searching, such as in DNA sequence alignment and data compression algorithms.
- **Range Queries and Updates**: Both segment trees and Fenwick trees are commonly used in problems involving dynamic range queries (e.g., finding the sum or minimum in a range) and updates (e.g., modifying an element in the array).
- **Gaming and Real-Time Systems**: Segment trees and Fenwick trees are used for efficiently processing dynamic events, such as updating scores or queries in online games.

These advanced data structures provide **time and space optimizations** for complex problems, making them indispensable in many real-world applications, particularly in **competitive programming**, **database indexing**, **signal processing**, and **real-time systems**.

Summary of Key Concepts:

- **Suffix Arrays**: Efficient for string processing problems, allowing for fast substring searches and pattern matching.

- **Segment Trees**: Ideal for problems involving dynamic range queries and updates, such as range sum, range minimum, and range maximum queries.

- **Fenwick Trees (Binary Indexed Trees)**: Used for efficient prefix sum queries and dynamic updates in a space-efficient manner.

- **Optimization**: These data structures enable optimization in space and time complexity, especially for large datasets and real-time applications.

CHAPTER 23

STRING MATCHING ALGORITHMS

In this chapter, we will explore **string matching algorithms**, which are essential for searching for patterns (or substrings) within a larger text. String matching is used in a wide variety of applications, from text editors and search engines to bioinformatics and DNA sequence analysis. We will cover some popular string matching algorithms, including the **Knuth-Morris-Pratt (KMP)** algorithm, the **Rabin-Karp** algorithm, and other **advanced pattern matching techniques**.

Introduction to String Matching Algorithms

String matching algorithms are used to find occurrences of a **pattern** (substring) within a **text** (larger string). The goal of these algorithms is to do so efficiently, especially when dealing with large texts or multiple pattern searches. A good string matching algorithm should ideally minimize the number of character comparisons and make use of previously gathered information about the text or pattern.

Some well-known string matching algorithms include:

1. **Knuth-Morris-Pratt (KMP)**: This algorithm preprocesses the pattern to build a **partial match** table, which helps skip unnecessary comparisons.

2. **Rabin-Karp**: This algorithm uses hashing to compare substrings of the text and pattern, enabling fast string matching for multiple patterns.

3. **Boyer-Moore**: A highly efficient string-matching algorithm that compares characters starting from the end of the pattern.

4. **Z-Algorithm**: A linear-time algorithm for pattern matching.

Knuth-Morris-Pratt (KMP) Algorithm

The **KMP algorithm** is an efficient string-matching algorithm that preprocesses the pattern to avoid unnecessary comparisons. It uses a partial match (or "prefix") table to store the lengths of the longest proper prefixes of substrings that are also suffixes.

Key Features:

- **Preprocessing**: The KMP algorithm preprocesses the pattern in $O(m)$ time, where m is the length of the pattern.
- **Matching**: The actual string matching is done in $O(n)$ time, where n is the length of the text.
- **Efficiency**: It avoids re-checking characters in the text that have already been matched with the pattern.

KMP Algorithm Steps:

1. **Preprocessing**: Create a **partial match table** (also called the "failure function") for the pattern. This table helps to skip over unnecessary characters when a mismatch occurs.

2. **Matching**: Traverse the text and compare characters with the pattern, using the failure function to skip ahead in the pattern when a mismatch occurs.

C++ Code for KMP Algorithm:

cpp

```
#include <iostream>
#include <vector>
using namespace std;

vector<int> computeLPS(string pattern) {
    int m = pattern.length();
    vector<int> lps(m, 0);   // Longest Prefix
Suffix array
    int length = 0;   // Length of the previous
longest prefix suffix
    int i = 1;

    while (i < m) {
        if (pattern[i] == pattern[length]) {
            length++;
```

```
            lps[i] = length;
            i++;
        } else {
            if (length != 0) {
                length = lps[length - 1];
            } else {
                lps[i] = 0;
                i++;
            }
        }
    }
    return lps;
}


void KMP(string text, string pattern) {
    int n = text.length();
    int m = pattern.length();

    vector<int> lps = computeLPS(pattern);   // Preprocess pattern
    int i = 0, j = 0;   // i for text, j for pattern

    while (i < n) {
        if (text[i] == pattern[j]) {
            i++;
            j++;
        }
        if (j == m) {
```

```
            cout << "Pattern found at index " <<
i - j << endl;
            j = lps[j - 1];   // Continue search
for next occurrence
        } else if (i < n && text[i] != pattern[j])
{
            if (j != 0) {
                j = lps[j - 1];   // Skip to the
next longest prefix suffix
            } else {
                i++;
            }
        }
    }
}


int main() {
    string text = "ABABDABACDABABCABAB";
    string pattern = "ABABCABAB";

    KMP(text, pattern);

    return 0;
}
```

Explanation:

- **computeLPS** function builds the "Longest Prefix Suffix" array, which tells us how much we can skip in the pattern when a mismatch occurs.
- The **KMP** function iterates over the text and uses the **LPS array** to avoid redundant comparisons.

Time Complexity:

- **Preprocessing**: O(m), where m is the length of the pattern.
- **Matching**: O(n), where n is the length of the text. Thus, the total time complexity is **O(n + m)**.

Rabin-Karp Algorithm

The **Rabin-Karp algorithm** is a string matching algorithm that uses **hashing** to find a pattern in a text. The idea is to compute the hash of the pattern and compare it with the hash of substrings of the text. If the hashes match, the algorithm checks the actual substring to confirm the match.

Key Features:

- **Hashing**: Rabin-Karp uses a hash function to map substrings to hash values.
- **Efficiency**: It performs **O(n)** time complexity on average when searching for a single pattern. However, in the worst case (due to hash collisions), it can take **O(n * m)** time, where m is the length of the pattern.

266

- **Multiple Patterns**: Rabin-Karp is especially efficient for searching for multiple patterns at once by computing a single hash table for all patterns.

Rabin-Karp Algorithm Steps:

1. Compute the hash value for the pattern.
2. Compute the hash value for substrings of the text with the same length as the pattern.
3. If the hash values match, check the actual characters in the substring to verify the match.

C++ Code for Rabin-Karp Algorithm:

cpp

```cpp
#include <iostream>
#include <string>
using namespace std;

const int d = 256;   // Number of characters in
the input alphabet
const int q = 101;   // A prime number for hashing

void rabinKarp(string text, string pattern) {
    int n = text.length();
    int m = pattern.length();
    int i, j;
```

```
    int patternHash = 0;      // Hash value for
pattern
    int textHash = 0;       // Hash value for text
    int h = 1;               // The value of d^(m-
1)

    // Precompute d^(m-1) for use in calculating
the hash values
    for (i = 0; i < m - 1; i++) {
        h = (h * d) % q;
    }

    // Calculate the hash value for the pattern
and first window of text
    for (i = 0; i < m; i++) {
        patternHash  =  (d  *  patternHash  +
pattern[i]) % q;
        textHash = (d * textHash + text[i]) % q;
    }

    // Slide the pattern over the text and check
for matches
    for (i = 0; i <= n - m; i++) {
        // If hash values match, check the actual
characters
        if (patternHash == textHash) {
            for (j = 0; j < m; j++) {
                if (text[i + j] != pattern[j])
break;
```

```
        }
        if (j == m) cout << "Pattern found at
index " << i << endl;
    }


    // Calculate the hash value for the next
window of text
        if (i < n - m) {
            textHash = (d * (textHash - text[i]
* h) + text[i + m]) % q;
            if (textHash < 0) textHash =
(textHash + q);  // Make sure it's positive
        }
    }
}


int main() {
    string text = "GEEKSFORGEEKS";
    string pattern = "GEEK";
    rabinKarp(text, pattern);
    return 0;
}
```

Explanation:

- The hash value for the pattern and each substring of the text is computed using a rolling hash function.
- If a match is found, the actual characters are compared to avoid false positives from hash collisions.

269

Time Complexity:

- **Average Case**: $O(n + m)$, where n is the length of the text and m is the length of the pattern.
- **Worst Case**: $O(n * m)$, due to hash collisions.

Advanced Pattern Matching Techniques

Besides KMP and Rabin-Karp, other advanced pattern matching algorithms include:

1. **Boyer-Moore Algorithm**:
   - This is a highly efficient string-matching algorithm, especially for large texts. It preprocesses the pattern to create two arrays (bad character and good suffix), which are used to skip over unnecessary comparisons, resulting in faster search times.
   - **Time Complexity**: Best case $O(n/m)$ and worst case $O(n * m)$.
2. **Z-Algorithm**:
   - The **Z-Algorithm** is used to preprocess a string to find all occurrences of a pattern in linear time $O(n + m)$. It computes the Z-array, which stores the lengths of the longest substrings starting from each position that are also prefixes of the string.

o   **Time Complexity**: O(n + m), where n is the length of the text and m is the length of the pattern.

3. **Aho-Corasick Algorithm**:

    o   The **Aho-Corasick algorithm** is a multi-pattern matching algorithm that uses a **trie** to store patterns and builds failure links to optimize matching. It is particularly effective when searching for multiple patterns at once.

    o   **Time Complexity**: O(n + k), where n is the length of the text and k is the number of patterns.

Summary of Key Concepts:

- **Knuth-Morris-Pratt (KMP)**: Efficient string matching using a **prefix function** to avoid redundant comparisons.
- **Rabin-Karp**: Uses **hashing** to find matches quickly, especially useful for searching multiple patterns.
- **Boyer-Moore**: A highly efficient pattern matching algorithm that skips unnecessary comparisons based on preprocessed information.
- **Z-Algorithm**: Linear time string matching algorithm that computes the **Z-array** for fast pattern matching.
- **Aho-Corasick**: Efficient multi-pattern matching using a **trie** and **failure links**.

String matching algorithms are essential in many fields, including text search, pattern recognition, bioinformatics, and data compression. Each algorithm has its strengths and is chosen based on the problem's requirements, such as the size of the text, the number of patterns, or the need for efficiency. Let me know if you'd like further details or more examples!

CHAPTER 24

COMPUTATIONAL GEOMETRY ALGORITHMS

In this chapter, we will explore **computational geometry**, a branch of computer science that deals with algorithms and data structures for solving geometric problems. These problems typically involve points, lines, polygons, and other geometric objects. Computational geometry plays a key role in various applications such as computer graphics, geographic information systems (GIS), robotics, and pattern recognition.

We will discuss some fundamental algorithms in computational geometry, including **convex hull algorithms**, **range queries**, and **line segment intersection**. These algorithms are essential for many geometric tasks, such as finding the boundary of a set of points, answering geometric queries efficiently, and detecting intersections in geometric shapes.

Introduction to Computational Geometry

Computational geometry involves the design and analysis of algorithms that deal with geometric objects. The goal is to develop efficient methods for solving geometric problems that arise in various applications. These algorithms typically involve

273

geometric shapes such as points, lines, line segments, polygons, and circles.

Some key problems in computational geometry include:

- **Convex Hull**: Finding the smallest convex polygon that encloses a set of points.
- **Line Segment Intersection**: Determining if two line segments intersect and, if so, finding the point of intersection.
- **Range Queries**: Efficiently answering queries about geometric objects within a given region.

We will look at some of these problems in detail and explore their solutions through algorithms.

Convex Hull Algorithms

The **convex hull** of a set of points is the smallest convex polygon that contains all the points. It is a fundamental problem in computational geometry, as the convex hull is often used as a preprocessing step for more complex geometric algorithms.

Convex Hull Definition:

- The convex hull of a set of points is the "tightest" polygon that can be formed such that all the points lie inside or on the boundary of the polygon.

- The convex hull can be visualized as the shape formed by a rubber band stretched around the set of points.

Convex Hull Algorithms:

1. **Graham's Scan Algorithm**:
   - This algorithm sorts the points based on their polar angle relative to the leftmost point and then constructs the convex hull by iterating over the sorted points and maintaining a stack of points.
   - **Time Complexity**: O(n log n), where n is the number of points.

2. **Jarvis's March Algorithm** (also known as the **Gift Wrapping** algorithm):
   - This algorithm starts from the leftmost point and wraps around the set of points, always selecting the next point that is the most counter-clockwise relative to the current point.
   - **Time Complexity**: O(nh), where h is the number of points in the convex hull and n is the total number of points.

C++ Code for Graham's Scan Algorithm:

cpp

```
#include <iostream>
#include <vector>
```

```cpp
#include <algorithm>
using namespace std;

struct Point {
    int x, y;
};

bool compare(Point p1, Point p2) {
    return p1.x < p2.x || (p1.x == p2.x && p1.y
< p2.y);
}

int orientation(Point p, Point q, Point r) {
    int val = (q.y - p.y) * (r.x - q.x) - (q.x -
p.x) * (r.y - q.y);
    return (val == 0) ? 0 : (val > 0) ? 1 : 2;
}

vector<Point> convexHull(vector<Point>& points)
{
    int n = points.size();
    if (n < 3) return {};

    sort(points.begin(), points.end(), compare);

    vector<Point> hull;

    // Lower hull
    for (int i = 0; i < n; i++) {
```

```
        while      (hull.size()    >=    2    &&
orientation(hull[hull.size() - 2], hull.back(),
points[i]) != 2)
            hull.pop_back();
        hull.push_back(points[i]);
    }


    // Upper hull
    int t = hull.size() + 1;
    for (int i = n - 2; i >= 0; i--) {
        while      (hull.size()    >=    t    &&
orientation(hull[hull.size() - 2], hull.back(),
points[i]) != 2)
            hull.pop_back();
        hull.push_back(points[i]);
    }


    hull.pop_back(); // Remove the last point
because it is repeated at the beginning


    return hull;
}


int main() {
    vector<Point> points = {{0, 0}, {1, 1}, {2,
2}, {3, 3}, {0, 3}, {3, 0}};


    vector<Point> hull = convexHull(points);
```

```cpp
    cout << "Convex Hull: ";
    for (auto& p : hull) {
        cout << "(" << p.x << ", " << p.y << ") ";
    }
    cout << endl;

    return 0;
}
```

Explanation:

- The algorithm first sorts the points based on their coordinates.
- It then iterates through the sorted points to construct the lower and upper hulls.
- The `orientation` function helps determine whether the turn between three points is clockwise, counter-clockwise, or collinear.

Time Complexity: O(n log n) due to sorting the points, followed by O(n) for constructing the convex hull.

Range Queries and Line Segment Intersection

1. Range Queries

Range queries involve answering questions about a set of geometric objects within a certain range. For example, you might need to find the minimum or maximum value of elements in a specific range or determine how many points lie within a given region.

A **range query** can be solved efficiently using **range trees** or **segment trees**. These data structures allow you to preprocess the data and answer queries in logarithmic time.

2. Line Segment Intersection

The **line segment intersection problem** involves determining whether two line segments intersect and finding the point of intersection, if any. This problem has many applications in computer graphics, geometric algorithms, and computational geometry.

Naive Approach:

- A simple way to check if two line segments intersect is by using the **orientation** of the points (similar to the convex hull algorithm).
- Two line segments (p1, q1) and (p2, q2) intersect if and only if the points (p1, q1) and (p2, q2) have opposite orientations with respect to each other.

C++ Code for Line Segment Intersection:

cpp

```cpp
#include <iostream>
using namespace std;

struct Point {
    int x, y;
};

int orientation(Point p, Point q, Point r) {
    int val = (q.y - p.y) * (r.x - q.x) - (q.x -
p.x) * (r.y - q.y);
    return (val == 0) ? 0 : (val > 0) ? 1 : 2;
}

bool onSegment(Point p, Point q, Point r) {
    return q.x <= max(p.x, r.x) && q.x >=
min(p.x, r.x) && q.y <= max(p.y, r.y) && q.y >=
min(p.y, r.y);
}

bool doIntersect(Point p1, Point q1, Point p2,
Point q2) {
    int o1 = orientation(p1, q1, p2);
    int o2 = orientation(p1, q1, q2);
    int o3 = orientation(p2, q2, p1);
    int o4 = orientation(p2, q2, q1);

    if (o1 != o2 && o3 != o4) return true;
```

```
    if (o1 == 0 && onSegment(p1, p2, q1)) return
true;
    if (o2 == 0 && onSegment(p1, q2, q1)) return
true;
    if (o3 == 0 && onSegment(p2, p1, q2)) return
true;
    if (o4 == 0 && onSegment(p2, q1, q2)) return
true;

    return false;
}

int main() {
    Point p1 = {1, 1}, q1 = {10, 1};
    Point p2 = {1, 2}, q2 = {10, 2};

    if (doIntersect(p1, q1, p2, q2)) {
        cout << "The line segments intersect." <<
endl;
    } else {
        cout << "The line segments do not
intersect." << endl;
    }

    return 0;
}
```

Explanation:

- The `orientation` function calculates the orientation of three points (whether they are collinear, clockwise, or counter-clockwise).

- The `doIntersect` function checks whether two line segments intersect by checking their orientations and ensuring that they do not lie on the same line (using the `onSegment` function).

Time Complexity: O(1) for checking if two line segments intersect.

Applications of Computational Geometry

1. **Computer Graphics**: Algorithms for finding intersections between line segments are used in ray tracing, collision detection, and other graphical applications.

2. **Geographic Information Systems (GIS)**: Range queries and convex hull algorithms are used in geographic mapping, spatial data indexing, and terrain analysis.

3. **Robotics**: Computational geometry is used for motion planning, pathfinding, and obstacle avoidance.

4. **Pattern Recognition**: Convex hulls are used in shape recognition and object detection.

5. **Network Design**: Algorithms for range queries and segment intersections are applied in network design, routing, and optimization problems.

Summary of Key Concepts:

- **Convex Hull Algorithms**: Used to find the smallest convex polygon enclosing a set of points. Common algorithms include Graham's scan and Jarvis's march.
- **Range Queries**: Efficiently answering queries about geometric objects within a specific region using range trees or segment trees.
- **Line Segment Intersection**: Determining if two line segments intersect, which is crucial for geometric applications like graphics, mapping, and robotics.

Computational geometry is a vast and powerful field that underpins many modern algorithms and applications, particularly in fields like computer graphics, robotics, and geographic information systems. Let me know if you'd like more examples or further explanations on any of these concepts!

CHAPTER 25

AMORTIZED ANALYSIS AND ADVANCED TIME COMPLEXITY

In this chapter, we will explore **amortized analysis** and **advanced time complexity**, which are crucial concepts for analyzing the performance of algorithms. Amortized analysis helps us understand the average time complexity of operations over a sequence of operations, particularly when some operations are costly, but their effects are spread out over many cheaper operations. We will also examine real-world examples where amortized analysis is applied and discuss how to optimize algorithms based on time complexity.

Understanding Amortized Analysis

Amortized analysis is a technique used to analyze the average time complexity of an algorithm over a sequence of operations, rather than just considering the worst-case time complexity of individual operations. This analysis is particularly useful when an algorithm involves a series of operations that have varying costs. While some operations may take a long time (in the worst case), others may be very efficient, and amortized analysis allows us to account for these variations.

The key idea behind amortized analysis is that the **cost of expensive operations can be spread out over many cheaper operations**, so the average cost per operation can be much lower than the worst-case cost for a single operation.

There are three common methods for performing amortized analysis:

1. **Aggregate Analysis**: This method calculates the total cost of a sequence of operations and divides it by the number of operations to find the average cost.

2. **Accounting Method**: In this method, we assign a "charge" or "credit" to each operation, sometimes including "extra credits" that are carried over to pay for more expensive operations in the future.

3. **Potential Method**: This method introduces a "potential function" that tracks the state of the data structure and reflects its "stored work." The difference in potential before and after an operation gives the amortized cost of that operation.

Real-World Examples of Amortized Analysis

Let's explore a few examples where amortized analysis is used to optimize algorithms.

1. Dynamic Arrays (Resizing Arrays)

One of the classic examples of amortized analysis is the **dynamic array** (like `std::vector` in C++). A dynamic array resizes itself when it runs out of space. Initially, the array has a small size, but when the array fills up, it must allocate more space to accommodate additional elements.

- **Expensive Operation**: The resize operation, which occurs when the array is full, requires ing all the elements to a new array with double the size. This operation takes **O(n)** time, where n is the number of elements in the array.
- **Cheap Operations**: Insertion of elements, when there is enough space, takes **O(1)** time on average.

Amortized Analysis of Dynamic Arrays:

Over a sequence of n insertions, the resize operation will happen **log n** times, and each resize operation will take **O(n)** time, where n is the number of elements. However, since each doubling only happens after a large number of insertions, the total cost of the **n** insertions is spread over multiple operations.

- The cost of the **i-th** insertion, when we reach a resize, is proportional to the total number of previous operations.
- Amortized time complexity for **n** insertions is **O(n)** because the total cost is spread across all the operations.

In this case, the amortized cost per operation is **O(1)**, even though the worst-case cost of a resize operation is **O(n)**.

2. Stack Operations (Push and Pop with Dynamic Resizing)

Consider a **stack** that dynamically resizes its array to store elements. Initially, the stack is small, but when it overflows, it is resized. Every time the stack is resized, the elements are copied to a new array, and that operation takes **O(n)** time. However, the amortized cost of the push operation is still **O(1)**, because the resizing occurs only occasionally, and the cost is spread out over multiple pushes.

3. Fibonacci Heap Operations

A **fibonacci heap** is a more advanced data structure used for priority queues, and it has a series of operations that have **amortized time complexity** that is much better than the worst-case time complexity of traditional heap implementations. For example:

- **Insert** operation: O(1) amortized
- **Delete-Min** operation: O(log n) amortized
- **Decrease-Key** operation: O(1) amortized

By using amortized analysis, Fibonacci heaps optimize time complexity for operations such as **decrease key** in Dijkstra's algorithm, which can significantly improve performance compared to traditional binary heaps.

Optimizing Algorithms Based on Time Complexity

Optimization based on time complexity involves identifying parts of an algorithm or data structure that can be made more efficient, particularly by reducing the time complexity of expensive operations.

1. Binary Search Trees (BSTs)

In a **binary search tree**, operations like **insertion, deletion**, and **search** typically have **O(log n)** time complexity when the tree is balanced. However, if the tree is unbalanced (e.g., a degenerate tree), these operations can degrade to **O(n)** time complexity.

- **Balancing the BST**: By using self-balancing trees such as **AVL trees** or **Red-Black trees**, we ensure that the tree remains balanced, which guarantees **O(log n)** time complexity for all operations.
- **Optimization**: The key to optimizing binary search trees is maintaining balance after each operation, which can be achieved through rotations or color changes in the case of Red-Black trees.

2. Hash Tables

Hash tables are used for fast lookups, insertions, and deletions. In theory, these operations have an **O(1)** time complexity. However, this can degrade if there are hash collisions or if the load factor becomes too high.

- **Optimization**: To optimize hash table operations, the hash function must be chosen carefully to minimize collisions, and **rehashing** is performed when the table exceeds a certain load factor to maintain an average **O(1)** time complexity.

3. Divide and Conquer Algorithms

Divide and conquer algorithms, such as **merge sort** and **quick sort**, often have a time complexity of **O(n log n)**. However, they can be optimized further by reducing the overhead associated with recursive calls or by using non-recursive implementations.

- **Tail Recursion Optimization**: Some algorithms can be optimized by eliminating the overhead of recursive function calls through **tail recursion optimization**.
- **Hybrid Sorting Algorithms**: Hybrid algorithms like **intro sort** (which combines quicksort, heapsort, and insertion sort) can be used to ensure optimal performance across a wide range of data types and sizes.

4. Dynamic Programming vs Greedy Algorithms

In many optimization problems, we need to choose between a **dynamic programming (DP)** approach and a **greedy algorithm**:

- **Dynamic Programming**: DP is generally used for problems where decisions depend on previous subproblems, and the goal is to find an optimal solution. DP often uses $O(n^2)$ or $O(n^3)$ time complexity, but the amortized cost of making decisions over time can reduce the overall cost.
- **Greedy Algorithms**: Greedy algorithms are faster because they make the locally optimal choice at each step. However, greedy algorithms may not always produce the globally optimal solution, so they must be used in the right context.

Optimization Tip: Always analyze the problem carefully before choosing between greedy and dynamic programming solutions. Greedy algorithms tend to be more efficient in terms of time complexity, but DP is preferred for problems with overlapping subproblems.

Summary of Key Concepts:

1. **Amortized Analysis**: A technique for analyzing the average time complexity of operations over a sequence of operations, often used when some operations are

expensive but spread out over many cheap operations. Common methods include **aggregate analysis**, **accounting method**, and **potential method**.

2. **Dynamic Arrays**: Amortized analysis shows that the average time for an insertion operation in a dynamic array is **O(1)**, even though resizing can take **O(n)** time in the worst case.

3. **Binary Search Trees**: Maintaining balance through techniques like AVL or Red-Black trees optimizes operations, ensuring **O(log n)** time complexity for insertions, deletions, and searches.

4. **Fibonacci Heaps**: Provide amortized **O(1)** time for insertion and **O(log n)** for **delete-min**, making them ideal for graph algorithms like Dijkstra's algorithm.

5. **Optimizing Algorithms**: Optimization based on time complexity involves choosing the right data structure, reducing overheads, and using hybrid approaches to improve efficiency (e.g., **intro sort**).

By carefully applying amortized analysis and optimizing algorithms based on time complexity, we can significantly improve the performance of algorithms, especially in large-scale or real-time applications. Let me know if you'd like further explanations or examples of specific optimizations!

CHAPTER 26

PARALLEL AND CONCURRENT ALGORITHMS

In this chapter, we will explore **parallel and concurrent algorithms**, which are key techniques for improving the performance and scalability of algorithms. By dividing tasks into smaller sub-tasks that can be executed simultaneously, parallelism and concurrency enable algorithms to take full advantage of modern multi-core processors. We will discuss the principles behind parallelism, how to implement parallel algorithms using **multithreading** in **C++**, and how to optimize algorithms for efficient parallel execution.

Introduction to Parallelism in Algorithms

Parallelism in algorithms refers to the ability to execute multiple operations at the same time. This is particularly useful when dealing with large datasets or computationally intensive tasks, as it allows the work to be split into smaller tasks that can be processed simultaneously, reducing the overall execution time.

There are two main types of parallelism:

1. **Data Parallelism**: This involves performing the same operation on multiple data elements simultaneously. For example, performing arithmetic operations on large arrays or matrices can be parallelized by dividing the array into chunks and processing each chunk in parallel.

2. **Task Parallelism**: This involves executing different tasks in parallel that may not necessarily be the same operation. For example, in a map-reduce operation, tasks can be divided into independent tasks that can be executed simultaneously.

Parallel algorithms aim to break a problem into smaller independent tasks, execute them concurrently, and combine the results efficiently. This is especially beneficial for problems that can be divided into independent subproblems that can be solved simultaneously.

Multithreading in C++

Multithreading is a key component of parallel computing. In **C++**, multithreading allows multiple threads of execution to run concurrently within the same program. The C++ Standard Library offers a thread class (since C++11) for creating and managing threads.

Key Concepts:

- **Thread**: A thread is a lightweight unit of execution within a process. A single process can have multiple threads running concurrently.
- **Mutex**: A mutex (short for "mutual exclusion") is used to prevent multiple threads from accessing shared data at the same time, avoiding race conditions.
- **Condition Variable**: A condition variable allows threads to wait for certain conditions to be met before continuing execution.

Multithreading Example in C++

Let's implement a simple **multithreading example** where we calculate the sum of an array in parallel using multiple threads.

cpp

```cpp
#include <iostream>
#include <vector>
#include <thread>
#include <atomic>
using namespace std;

void sumPartialArray(const vector<int>& arr, int
start, int end, atomic<int>& result) {
    int localSum = 0;
    for (int i = start; i < end; i++) {
```

```cpp
        localSum += arr[i];
    }
    result += localSum;  // Add local sum to the
atomic result
}


int main() {
    vector<int> arr = {1, 2, 3, 4, 5, 6, 7, 8, 9,
10};
    int n = arr.size();

    // Number of threads to use
    int numThreads = 2;
    atomic<int> result(0);   // To store the
result of the sum

    // Divide the array into sections for each
thread
    vector<thread> threads;
    int chunkSize = n / numThreads;

    for (int i = 0; i < numThreads; i++) {
        int start = i * chunkSize;
        int end = (i == numThreads - 1) ? n : (i
+ 1) * chunkSize;  // Handle last chunk

threads.push_back(thread(sumPartialArray,
ref(arr), start, end, ref(result)));
    }
```

```
// Wait for all threads to complete
for (auto& t : threads) {
    t.join();
}

cout << "Total sum: " << result.load() <<
endl;

return 0;
}
```

Explanation:

- We divide the array into **chunks**, each processed by a separate thread.
- We use an `atomic<int>` to safely update the result without causing race conditions.
- The `thread` class is used to create threads that run the `sumPartialArray` function concurrently on different chunks of the array.

Time Complexity:

- The time complexity for this operation is reduced from **O(n)** (for a single thread) to approximately **O(n / numThreads)** for each thread. The overall time complexity is proportional to **O(n)**, but the work is split across multiple threads.

Handling Concurrency and Synchronization

In parallel algorithms, proper synchronization is necessary to avoid **race conditions**, where multiple threads attempt to modify shared data simultaneously. The following synchronization mechanisms are commonly used in C++ multithreading:

- **Mutexes**: Protect shared resources to ensure only one thread can access them at a time.
- **Locks**: Use `std::lock_guard` or `std::unique_lock` for automatic locking and unlocking of mutexes.
- **Atomic Operations**: Use `std::atomic` for thread-safe operations without explicit locks, as demonstrated in the above example.

Optimizing Algorithms for Parallel Execution

To make the best use of parallel execution, algorithms should be designed in a way that allows tasks to be divided efficiently and processed concurrently. Here are some techniques for optimizing algorithms for parallel execution:

1. Divide and Conquer Algorithms

Divide and conquer algorithms are well-suited for parallel execution because they break a problem into independent subproblems that can be solved concurrently. For example, in **merge sort**, the two halves of the array can be sorted in parallel, and the merging process can also be parallelized.

2. Task Granularity

The size of the tasks that are being parallelized (i.e., **task granularity**) plays a significant role in the performance of parallel algorithms. If the tasks are too small, the overhead of managing threads can outweigh the benefits of parallelism. On the other hand, if tasks are too large, the load balancing might be suboptimal.

- **Optimal Granularity**: Tasks should be large enough to justify the parallel overhead, but small enough to ensure a balanced workload across threads.

3. Data Parallelism

Data parallelism involves applying the same operation to multiple data elements in parallel. For example, when performing element-wise addition on two large arrays, the operation can be done concurrently on each element. This is a natural fit for **SIMD**

(Single Instruction, Multiple Data) operations, which are supported by modern processors.

4. Load Balancing

Proper **load balancing** ensures that all threads perform an equal amount of work. This is particularly important in algorithms that divide the work unevenly, such as recursive algorithms. For instance, in parallel **quicksort**, ensuring that the pivot selection and partitioning work is evenly distributed across threads can improve performance.

5. Avoiding False Sharing

False sharing occurs when multiple threads access different variables that happen to be close together in memory, causing cache coherence issues. This can degrade performance. To avoid false sharing:

- Align data to cache boundaries.
- Use padding to ensure that frequently accessed variables are not on the same cache line.

Real-World Applications of Parallel Algorithms

1. **Multithreading in Web Servers**: Modern web servers handle multiple client requests concurrently using parallel algorithms. Each request can be processed by a separate

thread, improving the overall throughput and response time.

2. **Image and Video Processing**: Tasks like image filtering, edge detection, and video encoding/decoding can be parallelized by processing different parts of the image or video in parallel.

3. **Scientific Simulations**: Simulations, such as weather forecasting, fluid dynamics, and molecular modeling, often involve complex computations that can be parallelized for faster execution.

4. **Machine Learning**: Training large machine learning models involves many matrix operations, which can be parallelized using techniques like data parallelism and GPU-based computation.

Summary of Key Concepts:

1. **Parallelism** involves dividing tasks into smaller sub-tasks that can be executed concurrently to improve performance, especially on multi-core processors.

2. **Multithreading** in C++ allows concurrent execution of threads, enabling the parallelization of algorithms such as sorting and searching.

3. **Optimizing for Parallel Execution** requires dividing tasks efficiently (task granularity), ensuring proper synchronization (mutexes, locks, and atomic operations), and balancing the workload across threads.

4. **Real-World Applications** of parallel algorithms include web servers, image/video processing, scientific simulations, and machine learning, where large-scale problems can be solved more efficiently by leveraging parallel execution.

Parallel and concurrent algorithms are fundamental in modern computing, especially with the increasing importance of multi-core processors. By utilizing parallelism effectively, algorithms can be optimized to perform tasks faster and scale with larger datasets. Let me know if you'd like more examples or need further explanations on parallel programming!

CHAPTER 22

FINAL PROJECTS AND REAL-WORLD APPLICATIONS

In this chapter, we will explore how to apply the algorithms and techniques you've learned throughout your C++ programming journey to build **real-world projects**. These projects will involve integrating various **algorithms** and **data structures** and will serve as excellent examples of how C++ can be used in fields like **machine learning**, **game development**, and **networking**. We will also cover how to **troubleshoot** and **debug** C++ programs effectively to ensure that your projects run smoothly.

Building a Final Project Using C++ and Algorithms

When building a final project, it's important to select a problem or application that interests you and allows you to demonstrate your skills in using C++ algorithms and data structures. Below is a structured approach to building a comprehensive project:

1. Define the Project Scope

Before starting, it's essential to define the project's goals and requirements. Consider the following questions:

- **What problem are you solving?**
- **What algorithms and data structures will you need?**
- **What is the input and expected output?**
- **What is the scale of the project (small, medium, large)?**

Some project ideas might include:

- A **recommendation system** (using machine learning algorithms and data structures like trees and graphs).
- A **real-time multiplayer game** (using networking protocols and concurrency with multithreading).
- A **network router simulation** (using graph algorithms and network data structures).

2. Break the Project into Modules

Once you define the project, break it down into smaller, manageable modules. For example, if you're building a recommendation system:

- **Data Preprocessing**: Clean and prepare data for analysis.
- **Algorithm Design**: Implement recommendation algorithms (e.g., collaborative filtering, content-based filtering).
- **Interface**: Build a user interface (CLI or GUI).
- **Testing**: Write tests to ensure that the system works correctly.

303

3. Implementing the Solution

Start coding by implementing the algorithms and data structures you identified during the planning phase. Ensure that you:

- Use appropriate **C++ standard libraries** for efficient implementation (e.g., `vector`, `map`, `unordered_map`).
- **Modularize** your code to ensure that each component can be developed and tested independently.

Real-World Applications in Fields Like Machine Learning, Game Development, and Networking

1. Machine Learning

Machine learning (ML) is an area where C++ is widely used due to its performance and ability to handle large datasets efficiently. While Python has become the go-to language for ML, C++ is often used for performance-critical components like training algorithms or large-scale data processing.

Real-World Application:

- **K-Nearest Neighbors (KNN)** Algorithm in C++: The KNN algorithm is a simple classification algorithm that can be implemented using data structures like arrays and priority queues. A real-world project could involve building a KNN classifier that predicts the category of an item based on its nearest neighbors in a dataset.

304

- **Linear Regression**: C++ can be used to implement a linear regression model that learns the relationship between input and output variables.

Example of KNN Algorithm (simplified version):

cpp

```cpp
#include <iostream>
#include <vector>
#include <cmath>
#include <algorithm>

using namespace std;

struct Point {
    double x, y;   // Coordinates of the point
    int   label;           //  Class  label   (for
classification)
};

double euclideanDistance(const  Point&  a,  const
Point& b) {
    return sqrt(pow(a.x - b.x, 2) + pow(a.y -
b.y, 2));
}

int knn(const vector<Point>& data, const Point&
query, int k) {
```

```cpp
    vector<pair<double, int>> distances;

    // Calculate distance from the query point to
all other points
    for (const auto& point : data) {
        double dist = euclideanDistance(query,
point);
        distances.push_back({dist,
point.label});
    }

    // Sort distances to get the nearest
neighbors
    sort(distances.begin(), distances.end());

    // Count labels of the k nearest neighbors
    int countLabel1 = 0, countLabel2 = 0;
    for (int i = 0; i < k; i++) {
        if (distances[i].second == 1)
countLabel1++;
        else countLabel2++;
    }

    // Return the majority label
    return (countLabel1 > countLabel2) ? 1 : 2;
}

int main() {
    // Sample data
```

```
    vector<Point> data = {{1.0, 2.0, 1}, {2.0,
3.0, 1}, {3.0, 3.0, 2}, {6.0, 7.0, 2}};

    Point query = {3.0, 3.5};  // Query point

    int k = 3;
    int predictedLabel = knn(data, query, k);

    cout << "Predicted label: " << predictedLabel
<< endl;

    return 0;
}
```

2. Game Development

C++ is a preferred language in game development due to its efficiency, control over system resources, and support for high-performance graphics and real-time interactions. Many game engines, such as Unreal Engine, are built using C++.

Real-World Application:

- **Multiplayer Game Server**: Implement a real-time multiplayer game where players connect over the network and send commands to move characters. Use multithreading to handle multiple players simultaneously and design algorithms for **collision detection** or **game**

state synchronization using data structures like graphs or trees.

Basic Game Loop (simplified version):

cpp

```cpp
#include <iostream>
#include <thread>
#include <vector>
using namespace std;

void updateGameState(int playerId) {
    cout << "Player " << playerId << " is updating
their game state." << endl;
}

int main() {
    vector<thread> gameThreads;

    // Simulate 5 players
    for (int i = 1; i <= 5; ++i) {

gameThreads.push_back(thread(updateGameState,
i));
    }

    // Join threads to ensure they finish
    for (auto& t : gameThreads) {
```

```
        t.join();
    }


    cout << "All game states updated!" << endl;
    return 0;
}
```

In this example, each player updates their game state in parallel using **multithreading**.

3. Networking

Networking in C++ often involves building client-server applications, implementing protocols like TCP/IP, or using higher-level libraries such as **Boost.Asio**. Efficient data transmission and parallelism are critical when dealing with networking problems.

Real-World Application:

- **Network Packet Routing**: Implement a routing algorithm (e.g., **Dijkstra's shortest path**) for routing data packets across a network.
- **Chat Application**: Build a simple chat server and client, where multiple clients can communicate in real-time. Use multithreading to handle multiple clients at once.

Simple Chat Server with C++ (Multithreading):

```cpp
cpp

#include <iostream>
#include <thread>
#include <vector>
#include <mutex>
using namespace std;

mutex mtx;  // Mutex to synchronize chat messages

void handleClient(int clientId) {
    mtx.lock();
    cout << "Client " << clientId << " has sent
a message." << endl;
    mtx.unlock();
}

int main() {
    vector<thread> clients;

    // Simulate 5 clients sending messages
    for (int i = 1; i <= 5; ++i) {
        clients.push_back(thread(handleClient,
i));
    }

    // Join threads to ensure they finish
    for (auto& t : clients) {
        t.join();
```

```
    }

    cout  <<  "All  clients  have  sent  their
messages!" << endl;
    return 0;
}
```

In this simple example, each client is represented by a thread that sends a message, and **mutexes** ensure that the output is synchronized.

Troubleshooting and Debugging C++ Programs

When working with C++ projects, especially larger ones, **debugging and troubleshooting** are crucial steps to ensure that the program works correctly. Below are some strategies to help with debugging:

1. Use a Debugger

C++ provides powerful debuggers, such as **GDB** (GNU Debugger), that can be used to step through your code, inspect variables, and check for logical errors.

- **Breakpoints**: Set breakpoints to pause the program at specific locations and inspect the state.
- **Step Over**: Step through the code one line at a time to see how the program progresses.

- **Watch Variables**: Track the values of variables to see if they are updated correctly.

2. Add Logging

Adding logging statements (e.g., using `std::cout` or a logging library) can help you trace the program's execution and identify where things go wrong. This is especially useful for complex algorithms and multi-threaded programs.

3. Use Static Analysis Tools

Static analysis tools such as **Clang** or **Cppcheck** can analyze your code for potential bugs, memory leaks, and performance issues without running the program.

4. Handle Exceptions and Errors

Proper exception handling ensures that your program can recover gracefully from errors. Use `try-catch` blocks to handle runtime exceptions and avoid crashes.

5. Optimize for Performance

- Use **profilers** like **gprof** to identify performance bottlenecks.
- Make use of **C++11 and beyond** features (like move semantics and smart pointers) for memory efficiency.

- Utilize **multithreading** and parallelism, where appropriate, to speed up computationally expensive tasks.

Summary of Key Concepts:

1. **Final Projects**: Define a project's scope, break it down into manageable modules, and implement using C++ algorithms and data structures.

2. **Real-World Applications**:
   - **Machine Learning**: Implement algorithms like KNN or linear regression for predictions.
   - **Game Development**: Use multithreading for handling real-time multiplayer game states.
   - **Networking**: Build client-server applications, routing algorithms, and chat systems using C++.

3. **Troubleshooting and Debugging**: Use debuggers, logging, static analysis tools, and exception handling to identify and fix errors in C++ programs.

Building a project using C++ is a great way to demonstrate your understanding of algorithms, data structures, and programming techniques. By carefully planning, implementing, and debugging your project, you can create efficient and scalable solutions for real-world problems. Let me know if you need help with any specific project or debugging tips!

www.ingramcontent.com/pod-product-compliance
Lightning Source LLC
LaVergne TN
LVHW022335060326
832902LV00022B/4050

9 798280 240926